Introduction
to
Canoeing

Bradford Angier and Zack Taylor

Stackpole Books

INTRODUCTION TO CANOEING

Copyright © 1973 by
Bradford Angier and Zack Taylor
Published by
STACKPOLE BOOKS
Cameron and Kelker Streets
Harrisburg, Pa. 17105

Printed in the U.S.A.

Library of Congress Cataloging in Publication Data

Angier, Bradford.
  Introduction to canoeing.

  1. Canoes and canoeing. I. Taylor, Zack, joint author. II. Title.
GV783.A52   797.1'22   73-519
ISBN 0-8117-0912-4
ISBN 0-8117-2010-1 (pbk)

DEDICATION

For our canoeing wives, Vena and Sissy.

Contents

CHAPTER ONE

Choosing the Canoe

The North American Indians developed bark canoes, the forerunners of the present craft, using cedar, elm, chestnut, hickory, spruce, and birch barks. The lightness, toughness, and pliability of the latter soon established it as the best for the purpose. As for the word *canoe*, this evolved in the white tongues from the word *canaoa* which the rediscoverers of the New World heard in the West Indies. Today's sturdy, graceful canoes are actually the improved 20th Century models of the originally surprisingly functional Indian birch-bark boat.

No water craft has ever come near to the canoe for universal efficiency in lake and stream travel. Attractive, too, are its relatively low initial cost and upkeep—for with reasonable care the original purchase can be considered a lifetime investment—its light weight with the resultant ease of handling and in lifting it atop a car, its load-carrying capacity which is unusually high when compared to most boats of the same size, its versatility when used with a motor with which safe speeds near 10 miles an hour are attainable, and even its ability to sail well.

There are three very basic things any canoe can do that no other boats can accomplish. It can be easily portaged, as its cigar shape makes it simple for one or two men to handle. Any boat can be made lightweight, but the long graceful canoe shape assures its being the easiest of all boats to carry. Second, a canoe is one of the few small boats that are paddled without any inconvenience with the paddler looking ahead. In most other oar boats the person rowing faces aft. Third, the long graceful shape that is carried so easily happens by coincidence to be the shape that most easily slips through the water.

Canoes can and have been made out of every material one can think of; bone ribs and hides, rushes and bark and, of course, logs. They are the commonest craft in the world today. Variations and names are endless, but basically any long displacement hull propelled by people facing forward, and light enough to carry, is a canoe. Actually, the newest tankers follow basic canoe lines underwater. Bill Lapworth, designer of super-successful racing sailboats in the "Cal" series, says he just took a canoe shape and put a keel and spade rudder on it. Basically, the canoe is a flat-bottomed boat with hard bilges. Rounded bottoms come only on racing canoes.

The white men copied Indian canoes and perfected the lines in the voyageur trade. However, modern canoes all stem from the *Princess* class canoes as designed by the Honorable Nicholas Longworth, member of the old Cincinnati Canoe Club and commodore of the American Canoeing Association (1881-82), and built for the club in the 1880's by J. Henry Rushton, a noted New York State builder. Rushton's canoes won fame for beauty and performance. The models evoked Red Cross interest and appeared in their *Canoeing,* having by then achieved almost cast-in-bronze status. Grumman, when they went to their first aluminum canoes in 1948, blunted the bows and cut the end tops lower. This was a design breakthrough.

Now Ralph Sawyer, about 1968, put some of his racing knowledge into hull shapes and produced a boat that would go 6 miles per hour, versus a Grumman at 5 miles per hour, with the same power. Basically, the shape is slightly narrower, the ends finer, and the keel shaped from the sharpness of the bottom fore and aft. Others have copied these boats and gone off into new directions, with mostly longer and leaner canoes with a longer waterline that goes faster but sacrifices some load-carrying capacity. These boats, all fiberglas, are the way canoeing is headed, along with the new whitewater craft.

Load-carrying ability today isn't as important as it once was. First, equipment weighs much less. Think of today's pup tents versus the heavy old water-proofed canvas, freeze-dry versus canned stuff, even outboards. Then, too, much canoe-ing is with clubs, often with cars or powerboats in company. Third, there are fewer and fewer areas that far away from a supermarket. Sure, one might want a Grumman for two weeks in Algonquin National Park, but one doesn't need it for week-end jaunts. Here one will want to run rivers (whitewater boats) or lakes where speed and ease of pushing becomes vital.

Even the most up-to-the-minute, trailer-towing campers are learning that the canoe is an excellent and light car-topping addition to their camping outfits, especially when it comes to enjoying the multiple possibilities of the lakes and streams that are to be found at many campgrounds. The hunter and fisherman, as well as the plain ordinary wanderer, are dis-covering both near and remote country newly accessible to them with a canoe. Families are finding canoeing a unique and healthy pastime in which everyone can paddle and join in the fun, for not only is canoeing not a spectator sport, but there are few who sample it who do not become engrossed in the adventure and excitement it embraces.

The canoe is a vehicle that nearly everyone can learn to use safely and effectively in a comparatively brief time—with just a bit of instruction, printed or firsthand, plus common sense, practice, and reasonable recognition of certain basic rules of balance and steerage. Necessary first, though, is the right craft for the main intended uses.

FLAT OR ROUND BOTTOM?

Every line in a canoe is important. A flattish bottom, for example, is more stable than a round one. However, the round-bottomed canoe is swifter, at the same time responding more quickly to the paddle. These characteristics are offset, however, unless the purpose is racing, by the round-bottom's more limited capacity for the food and duffle needed on extended cruises.

Given a choice, the round bottom is superior in maneuverability and speed. The flatter bottom is more stable, because in a current this streamlines itself above the moving water rather than, as the round one does, settling the craft more deeply into the flow. Too, the flattish bottom can venture into shallower places. All in all, handling bulkier and heavier loads, it is the spirited work horse of the breed.

All this consideration of lines leads to the tumblehome, the term for the structurally strengthening inward-curving of the sides. Again, this feature is a matter for compromise. The voyager will be able to reach the water with his paddle easier and more effectively the more tumblehome there is. On the other hand, wave tops will slosh into the canoe less annoyingly when there is not so much tumblehome or when the sides even round outward.

The end shapes of canoes today are kept low to avoid windage and upswept only enough to give some more free-

STANDARD OR AVERAGE
ROUNDNESS TO BOTTOM

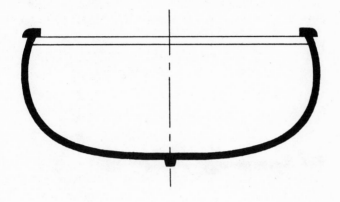

FAST AND TIPPY
DEEP AND ROUND
NO KEEL—GOOD FOR
WHITEWATER

Profiles—round vs. flat-bottomed canoes.

FLAT FREIGHT

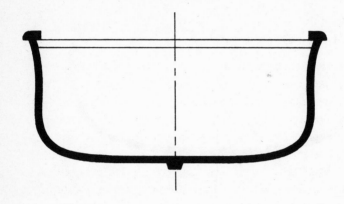

FULLY DECKED RACING CANOE
OR KAYAK
HULL
SHAPE

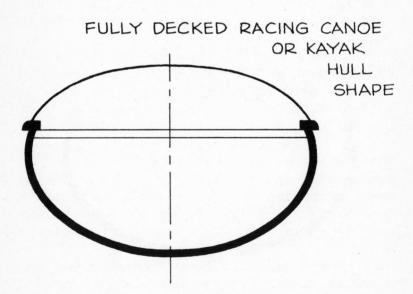

Profiles—round vs. flat-bottomed canoes (continued).

board at bow and stern. But the Indians everywhere kept the great high bows that must have been a nuisance in winds. Why? Probably purely for decoration. The various tribes wanted a place to paint their imaginative designs.

CHIEF USE—RIVER OR LAKE?

Whether or not a canoe is better suited for lake rather than river travel depends, too, on its lines. In this case those of the keel are particularly important. The keel, of course, is the bottom of the craft from bow to stern. When the keel is straight, the traveler will find he is better able to hold his course on a lake, any tendency to drift to the side being less.

On the other hand, when the keel line of the craft lifts at both ends, the canoe will be better able to spin on a dime, as it were, pivoting more promptly to follow a channel in rock-frothing rapids or swerving to avoid an upthrusting log. Such an uplifted bow and stern, so useful in swift water, become liabilities on lakes because of the sail-like way they catch the wind.

Then there is the matter of sharpness. Just as with the rounded bottom, the keener and less tapered the bow and stern, the faster the canoe will drive ahead and the easier it will be to paddle. Again, however, this means cutting down both on load-toting capacity and on seaworthiness.

The narrow bow knifes into waves rather than lifting over them. The narrow stern encourages following seas to splash into the canoe, especially when a heavy load has settled it deeply into the water. Unless the primary desire is for racing, then, the ride on both lakes and rivers will be sturdier and safer with a wider bow that carries its broadness well amidships.

At the other extreme, there is the flat stern, built to accommodate an outboard motor. This is all right for lake travel, although square sterns paddle about a mile an hour

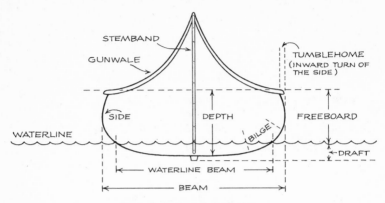

STEMBAND

GUNWALE

TUMBLEHOME
(INWARD TURN OF
THE SIDE)

SIDE   DEPTH   FREEBOARD

WATERLINE

BILGE

DRAFT

WATERLINE BEAM

BEAM

Canoe features and nomenclature.

slower because of the suction on the chopped transom. The way the pushing current builds up against such a stern in fast water, too, makes it unsuitable for river journeys. Here, if a kicker is wanted, the canoeist will do much better to use a standard canoe and one of the handy little motor mounting brackets that are inexpensively available. An exception is the stern whose flatness, large enough to accommodate the clamps of an outboard motor, does not extend below the water line.

The square-stern canoe is basically a displacement boat, although with a big motor the flat sections aft will tend to plane the craft. Still, power is severely restricted; about 5 hp maximum for 15 to 17-footers, 7.5 to 9 hp for 19-footers and larger. Speeds are less than 10 mph. The square-stern canoe is for mostly motor use but where one needs a boat that can be handled easily with paddles and is still conveniently portable.

Square sterns are generally recommended when an outboard motor, usually in the 1 to 9½ horsepower class, is to be used most of the time. For all-around canoeing, however, the double-end canoe is superior in handling qualities, one advantage being its ability to paddle effectively in either direc-

Using outboard on square-sterned canoe. Attaching the motor can be an awkward job. Some load or ballast also is needed forward to compensate for motor weight and for efficient cruising; the bow otherwise tends to ride too high.

tion. Double-end canoes generally float higher and, as a result, have more capacity.

The side motor-mounts that are securable for them offer a simple, effective, and safe method of operating a canoe with a small outboard motor, although a canoe with a side mount can capsize more easily than one with the motor attached to the stern. The side mount is more comfortable to use, despite the fact that an off-center shaft can upset the boat in too tight

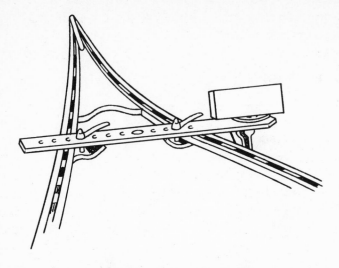

A typical side-mounting motor bracket.

Side-mounted motor in use. Motor control is more comfortable and convenient this way, but sudden, fast turns or the motor grounding can cause a capsize.

a turn. The stern mount crinks the neck and shoulders when one is steering long distances.

KEEL CHOICE

Keels themselves are also a matter of compromise. If much traveling on windy lakes is planned, even a keel no more than an inch deep, ridging the center of the bottom from bow to stern, will save a lot of side-slipping.

But many lake craft are also taken down streams, and there the current affects the keeled canoe more decisively, hindering for one thing the speed and ease with which the craft can be paddled or poled broadside when the occasion demands.

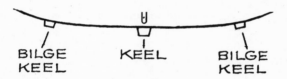

BILGE   KEEL   BILGE
KEEL   KEEL

Bottom profile illustrating added auxiliary keel shoes.

Yet a canoeist can get along in white water with a one-inch keel, especially one that tapers to a point at each end. This will have the added function of protecting the bottom to some extent from rocks and gravel.

In fact, river craft are frequently shod for protective purposes. Such wooden or metal strips, wider than they are deep, are often added by the owners of both canvas and wooden canoes, the center keel being screwed from bow to stern and the shorter auxiliary shoes attached parallel to this on both sides of the canoe bottom. Shoes of this sort, not high enough to cause too much difference in steerage, will absorb a lot of abrasion and abuse.

ORDINARY KEEL

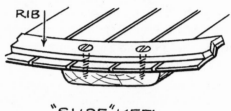

"SHOE" KEEL

Note shape of ordinary vs. "shoe" keels.

CANOE SIZE

If the buyer could load and man his prospective canoe before deciding on it, selection of the optimum size would be an easy matter. All he'd then have to do would be to pick the smallest and lightest craft so that when everyone and everything was aboard it still showed six inches of clearance amidships, between the water line and the top of the gunwale.

That's how much freeboard there should be for ideal maneuverability and safety. The reason one can't ordinarily play it conservatively and pick a craft that will surely be big enough for any contingency is that canoes, unlike most other watercraft, are regularly lifted manually from the water for transporting, portaging, and storing. In other words, the canoe must be as lightweight as practical.

For a canoe that is to be used by two or three individuals on small lakes, the 17-footer is an apt choice. Such a craft can be portaged by one man, as well as handily hoisted atop a car.

A canoe as short as 11 feet will ordinarily give one individual all the fishing, hunting, and short-term cruising he wants. But for trips on which enough food and gear for upwards of a week must be packed, or when a companion will be along, one will do better with at least a 14-footer.

There's also the consideration that, although lighter, the shorter canoes are not easier to handle in the water. Usually narrower, too, they float more cumbersomely when loaded and manned than do longer models. Balancing, also, becomes more touchy. In fact, if one can handle it, for all-around purposes he'll likely be happiest with a 17-foot or 18-foot canoe. Such a craft, depending on the material and when this can absorb water on dryness, will weigh from 60 to 85 pounds.

The shorter the canoe, the crankier it gets to paddle. Canoes with a longer waterline slide through the water easier and have more "shoot" after each stroke. The boats below 11 feet don't have this "shoot" as much. With them it is better to use a double-bladed paddle.

If two vacationists plan to take off for a month or more, they will be even better served with a 20-foot canoe. This will weigh about 125 pounds, and it'll normally require two to portage it, although each canoeist will probably be able to shoulder a packsack apiece at the same time.

Then there are the Far North's freight canoes, now being replaced more and more by planes. These big watercraft range upwards from 26 feet in length, weigh at a minimum some 160 pounds dry when made of wood and canvas, and readily handle a ton, especially when as is generally the case they are running the long flattish rivers of the region ahead of an outboard motor.

At the other extreme, Nessmuk—famous American woodsman of a century ago—traveled with a 17-pound canoe, the

Freight canoe.

Sairy Gamp—wryly named after the tippling nurse of Dickens' fame who "never took a drop of water." This craft was especially made for Nessmuk by J. Henry Rushton. It was later exhibited at the Columbian Exposition. During the first World War, W. Sterling Burgess, the yacht designer, borrowed it as a model for lifeboats in navy planes. It was finally acquired by the Smithsonian Institution in Washington, D.C., where it now rests.

"My own load including canoe, extra clothing, blanket-bed, two days' rations, rod and knapsack, never exceed 76 pounds," George Washington Sears, better known by the Indian name of Nessmuk, wrote in 1888; "and I went prepared to camp out any and every night. . . . My canoe is my yacht, as it would be were I a millionaire."

Old Town is now making a plastic copy of the early cedar-and-oak Nessmuk-Rushton pack canoes. An idea of how inflation has swelled the economy can be gained by the fact that whereas Rushton sold his featherweights for $27.50, Old Town at this writing lists $195 as the competitive price for the modern model.

This little one-man canoe, weighing only 18½ pounds, is best used by expert canoeists, its being necessarily fragile when compared to conventional craft despite a reasonable sturdiness and flexibility. Although enough of a two-inch-thick layer of polyvinyl Ethafoam has been cemented in to make the fly-weight unsinkable, wearing some sort of a life-preserver vest or such is still a sound safety precaution as, realistically, it is with any canoe.

ALUMINUM RATES A

The sleek, relatively safe and rugged, easily maintained aluminum canoe merits the satisfaction that keeps it outselling all other canoes in the United States by five to one. In fact, its good points are so well known that probably the best perspective can be gained by first considering its several shortcomings.

One of the characteristics the prospective canoeist has come to expect is quietness, especially when he's angling or hunting on still waters, or, in fact, when he just doesn't want to disturb the tranquility. The aluminum canoe, however, is noisy. Even when all contact between canoe and paddle is avoided, including the resounding scrape of haft against gunwale, and when no long-carrying boom announces the touching against rock or submerged log, there is still the staccato rap, rap, rapping of wavelets.

Like other metals, aluminum can become unbearably hot beneath the sun, then chillingly cold before freezeup and again when the ice is just out. It dents easily. Speaking scientifically, it does not slide through the water as sleekly as it might unless specially painted. This last is an easily overcome consideration, of course, but the aluminum canoe also has a tendency to adhere annoyingly to rocks with which it may come in contact. Simonize the bottom to fix this.

In mishaps, too, it has a sometimes dangerous tendency that one day might really leave the voyager up against it. Being closer to self-righting than the cedar-and-canvas breed, after capsizing it may far too readily follow the current beyond reach, or on a lake blow away before its recent occupants can get back to it, rendering futile or at the least inadvisable the former sound safety rule that in case of an upset one should always stick with the canoe.

On the other hand, a multitude of good points keep it the fastest selling of all new models in this country. Although inherently fragile like any other thin-skinned conveyance, including the family car, aluminum canoes are surprisingly sturdy. They are not too difficult to repair, both temporarily and later permanently, in case of the usual minor accident. They do not deteriorate the way a canvas-and-wood craft does, and with them one completely sidesteps that insidious enemy, dry rot.

They paddle sensitively and with beautiful responsiveness. They will not sink or absorb water and so grow heavier with the years. They are easy to store almost anywhere. Furthermore, good aluminum canoes are readily available, selling within a realistic price range when it is considered that when not too drastically abused one is good for the owner's lifetime. And any unpleasant reactions to their comparative noisiness generally disappear with experience.

For instance, there is the 17-foot Grumman Standard. The closing days of World War II caused the Grumman Aircraft Corporation to develop consumer products. In 1944 they started tooling on a new line of boats, specifically canoes. The first of these was a 17-footer designed along conventional lines, but fashioned from a relatively new material, marine aluminum. In November the first shipments went to 22 states and to the three-century-old Hudson's Bay Company in Canada.

Traditionalists took one look and raised howls of anguish. Where had gone the painstaking canoe workmanship, the exquisite curved ribbing, the shiny varnish, and the glossy sides? A canoe had been a thing of beauty, but this was a metal monster. No craftsman's hand lovingly built this boat! A machine stamped it out like a tin can.

Then some curious things began happening, or not happening. Alaska trappers ran Grumman Standards upstream, hitched their dogs to them, and used them as sleds. North Country game wardens left them in the bush and porcupines didn't chew them. White-water canoeists bounced the metal bottoms off rocks. The new boats would not only take twice or three times the punishment of a wooden canoe but ten times as much! Furthermore, the aluminum boats didn't cost or weigh any more than conventional canoes. Finally, maintenance wasn't just reduced; it was eliminated.

Men who judged boats not as furniture or pretty pictures, but for what they did and where they took one, gladly accepted the new design. By the middle of 1971 Grumman produced number 75,000 of this one model alone, making it easily America's most popular canoe.

Aluminum is by far the most common canoe material, Grumman the most popular make. Strength in an aluminum canoe comes from number of frames and skin thickness. A very strong canoe would be .073". Most standard aluminum canoes are .050" gauge. Grumman lightweights are .032" but have more frames; 17-ft. standard with 3 frames, 17-ft. lightweight with 7.

New unique canoes from Sportpal, Emlenton, Pa. use .023" and are the smallest and lightest for their size. The 12-footer weighs 29 lbs., costs $295; the 14-footer weighs 40 lbs. and sells for $334. Two tiny canoes just offered? Old Town has a 10½-footer weighing 19½ lbs. at $195. Sportspal has an 8-footer weighing 20 lbs. at $180. Old Town's tiny canoe is fiberglas; Sportspal is aluminum.

Aluminum in its natural state oxidizes a film of greyish white powder on the surface that actually protects the metal from further oxidation. This can be polished off with regular aluminum cleaners sold at trailer supply houses and in supermarkets. Marine aluminum lasts perfectly in salt water, and is an alloy of aluminum, magnesium, and chromium in varying amounts; magnesium mostly. Aluminum used in canoes stretches, which gives it greater strength, but makes repairing difficult if the stretch is great enough.

Aluminum canoes may start to leak around rivets. First remedy is to re-set the rivets; i.e., to try to pound them flatter and tighter. If this fails, chop heads and re-rivet with larger size.

Aluminum can be welded but it takes a real good man to do so. Around the keel area it may not even be possible to weld, as many manufacturers put a neoprene gasket under the keel to prevent leaks.

Attachments may be made to aluminum with stainless steel screws or bolts. Aluminum bolts are not strong enough, and brass and/or iron set up a metal corrosion. Stainless extrudings such as pads, straps, etc. last indefinitely.

Aluminum can be painted. A primer wash is first needed to raise a slight tooth on the metal. If originally painted by the manufacturer, the wash can be omitted, as a new paint coat will stick to the old. Paint will chip and scar, of course, but the new spray-can touch-up kits make keeping hull color fairly simple. Best way is to paint the outside of the hull only, leaving the interior metal bare, as the inside takes the hardest beating.

THE CANVAS CANOE—A VANISHING SPECIES?

Most popular still in Canada, accounting there for four out of every five sales, is the canvas-covered, cedar-strip canoe. This goes back to the latter half of the last century when cedar-strip crafts started replacing the wonderfully light and swift, but fragile and excessively perishable, birch bark canoe. Despite their sturdy advantages, however, these wooden craft had one serious drawback, a tendency to soak up excessive amounts of water which made them unduly heavy to portage.

The Chestnut Canoe Co. of Fredericton, New Brunswick, the grand-daddy of modern canoe manufacturers since its founding in 1897, licked this problem just before the turn of the century by adding a canvas covering. This, when adequately sized, would during a day's travel pick up no more than a few ounces of moisture, most of which evaporated when the craft was overturned for the night.

Improved still more during the past 75 years, these traditional wood-and-fabric canoes are today the choice of the purist, one of their selling points being the contention that they will pole more easily than their aluminum counterparts. Too, in an emergency the craft can be repaired with no more than a patch cut from the clothing and stuck on with spruce gum. And in one the traveler can satisfyingly paddle with almost complete silence through the quiet aisles.

Self-floating without the addition of air pockets or of air-holding plastics, the canvas-and-wood canoe, nevertheless, does have its own drawbacks, too. Not the least of these is that

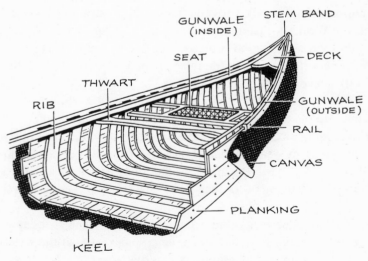

Cross-section, wood-canvas canoe construction.

it's more susceptible to damage than either the aluminum or the fiberglas vehicle. Too, this choice of many an experienced wilderness tripper and connoiseur is harder to maintain, although there is perhaps no feeling quite as rewarding as making a *new* canoe out of an old one in the springtime by scraping, sanding, repainting, and revarnishing.

FIBERGLAS CANOES

All the exciting new canoe shapes are fiberglas. These slimmer, lower-freeboard boats are faster with the same power, easier to control in a wind, and sleek and beautiful. All modern white-water canoes and kayaks, the so-called banana boats, are fiberglas.

It is easy to build a poor canoe out of the plastic fiberglas. The weakest reinforcing is mat, used on the exterior of hulls as it takes a super smooth surface. Then follows glass cloth. Now cloth comes in weights from 4 oz. per square yard to 20 oz. per square yard. Standard is 7.5 oz. The strongest reinforcement is called roving. This is like extra-heavy woven cloth. Weakest material is chopped matting, unfortunately often used as it can be sprayed from special guns. It is sound practice not to buy any fiberglas canoe that doesn't show the cloth weave on the inside.

Advantages of fiberglas are no maintenance. Hull color is built into the gel coat, although sometimes it is just painted on. Like aluminum, the plastic doesn't rot or corrode. It is fairly impervious to weather, does not range from hot to cold, and is silent. It is easily repaired by the amateur who just has to slop patches over cuts or tears. The new resins will adhere, and strength will be as great as before.

However, the biggest advantage of fiberglas canoes today is that more modern shapes are easier to push through the water than their standard aluminum counterparts.

CONSTRUCTION—THE DEBATE GOES ON

If one wants durability, buy aluminum. For speed and handling buy the comparatively priced plastic. Beware of so-called *budget* canoes. For tradition and beauty, the canvas-and-wood crafts are still supreme. In any event, purchase only the best, as a good canoe depreciates never more than about 50 percent —ever.

And so the debate goes on, but whatever choice the American or Canadian finally decides upon, one thing is certain— North America is filled with canoeing waters to satisfy every taste.

CHAPTER TWO

Paddles—Choice, Use and Care

"To have commanded the paddle, tasted the wind, and challenged the river—one would have believed that the splendor of God's wilderness is reserved for the canoeist."

So it goes. Man dueling with nature, taming mighty streams, extracting from a foreign and often excitingly hostile environment pleasure and satisfaction! More than that, triumph! There is something in everybody that cries out for the chance to pit brains and brawn against what can be merciless and deadly. That's what canoeing is all about, especially on the remoter waterways and the windier lakes.

One is permitted only the frailest of weapons. First comes a tiny boat, powered by the lightweight paddle in the canoeist's own hands. His tent is a scrap of fabric. A few pots and pans, a match, a compass, a fish line and lure. . . . These are weapons to conquer untamed waters, because the ages have fine-honed them to perfection. All they need is the essential requirement of acquired skill and they will quite literally carry one in safety and cheer to the ends of the earth, to El Dorado, to the unforgettable. Anyone can do it. Wheel-chair victims have canoed the wilderness. Wee wisps of girls manage it all the time. In a recent year no less than 134,000 individuals canoed the Quetico-Superior area alone, many with not a modicum of previous experience.

Admittedly, that isn't much of a sales talk—a little poetry, a few facts. But there is a heady elixir smoking from this bottle. Sniff it? Smells like balsam, doesn't it? And a river. Hear the wind? It swishes in the pines. See the fire embers glow. The sleeping bag is warm. Hear the rapids gurgle. They will sing all night long.

Is the medicine taking? Want to try it? Here's how, told as one will travel out there—lean and spare. Non-essentials not allowed!

Everything begins with the carefully chosen canoe, already considered. Next comes the paddle.

THE PARTICULAR PADDLE

In all the active sports such as tennis, golf, fishing, hunting, skiing, and the rest, the difference between a good and an inept performance often stems directly from the choice of the specific tool that is essential to the art. With canoeing, it's the paddle that is all important, particularly as during the usual day of cruising the ordinary American voyager will average about a stroke every two seconds, 30 a minute, 1800 an hour, and close to 15,000 during a bracing eight-hour day. Incidentally, this works out to somewhat less than 500 strokes a mile.

There is one interesting fact, though, gleaned from the Indians. A short, quick stroke eats up more miles with less expenditure of energy than the usual slow pace of some 25 to 30 strokes a minute. Try upping the pace to more like one stroke every 1⅓ seconds. To do this, the Indian concentrates his strength in the first part of the stroke. His power diminishes swiftly once the paddle is opposite his side, and he ends the stroke quickly after this point is passed, thus doing away with any tendency to pull down the stern rather than add to the onward motion.

In fact, with a sufficiently limber paddle, the spring of the shaft and blade themselves will do much to shoot the paddle forward for the next stroke with but little effort on the part of the canoeist. To accomplish this, the lower hand should be rigid at the end of the stroke and there should be a brief surge of renewed power just before the blade leaves the water.

In any event, paddle weight, grip, balance, shape, finish, material, and especially length are, therefore, all vital.

First of all, the paddle should fit the job, whether for bow or for stern work. For use up front in the canoe, where little if any steering will usually be done, the paddle should reach from the floor to the chin when the standing canoeist holds it in front of him.

The stern paddle, on the other hand, should be at least eye high. There are those, too, who like the stern paddle in particular to be a couple of inches longer than this standard, largely depending on the lines of the particular canoe and especially the tumblehome as considered in Chapter One. With this paddle, in any event, the individual in the back of the canoe will handle most of the steering and control.

The most important thing about a canoe paddle is seldom mentioned. That is, the paddle should be long enough so the man paddling does not have to bend down his back to make the stroke. The basic canoe paddling is done with shoulders and hips swinging, using the big muscles of legs and your back. What is not wanted is bending the back, hunching at every stroke. This makes paddle-length determination difficult.

For instance, if one paddles kneeling, the right paddle length will be different than if one will be paddling from a seat.

The best way to select the right length paddle is to experiment with various lengths. The length of the arms will figure in how long the paddle should be and even how far apart one will like to hold his hands. Commonly available lengths are: Old Town, 4′, 4′3″, 4′6″, 4′9″, 5′, 5′3″, 5′6″, 5′9″, and 6′; Grumman, 4′6″, 5′, 5′6″, and 6′.

There should be a third paddle for emergency use in each two-man canoe. It's very easy to lose a paddle, not to mention the danger of breaking one, and this spare should be carried wedged handily under the load lashings, ready to be grabbed in an instant by either paddler. When these two individuals are about the same height, the length of this extra paddle can well be a compromise between both's chin and eye measurements.

What about blade width? Discussion of this point has kept many a canoeist adding more logs to the night campfire. The craft will travel faster and answer steerage demands more agily with a wide paddle. On the other hand, it takes more strength and stamina to draw a wide blade through the water than it does to manipulate the often adequate narrow blade. The actual widths available today mostly straddle the fence between 5½ and 8 inches. When it comes to using one, a lot will depend on the individual's own muscles and physical condition. Naturally, the wider blades displace more water and make better time, at the same time requiring more effort. Those experts of experts, the American Indians, preferred the less tiring narrow blades.

Incidentally, if one of the two blades chosen is wider than the other, this should be in the stern paddle.

The canoeist should pick a paddle that feels comfortable and secure in his hands. Part of this will depend on the grip. Because it can be grabbed effectively from nearly every angle, the pear-shaped grip seen on most paddles is the most universally acceptable. Racers, who must hold the paddle even

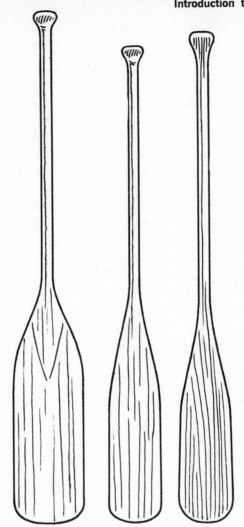

Canoe paddles. Widest paddle in any pair is used at stern.

more staunchly, generally seek a more abruptly angled T-grip
which, too, has its variations. Then there is the compromis-
ing rounded grip whose sides, usually thinned for extra resil-
iency, diminish gradually into the shaft itself. On some Indian

paddles there was no particular grip at all, just as there is none on a rake handle, but most modern canoeists shun such a paddle.

In any event, before one settles for any paddle he should hold it so that he can sight along the shaft toward the blade—just as the expert woodsman does before buying an ax—and make sure that the implement is straight all the way. Look, too, at the grain, being suspicious of any that are too thickly hidden by paint or varnish. This grain should also run straight if the paddle is to be true and durable.

Once one has purchased his paddles, unless blisters and slipperiness don't matter, it's a sound idea to take off any finish on the grips and shafts with sandpaper and if necessary a hardware-store solvent, leaving the protective varnish or paint on the blade. Soak the now exposed wood thoroughly in order to raise the grain, which should then be sanded smooth. Continue doing this until the wood remains smooth after soaking. Then, once everything is dry again, get the hands slick with boiled linseed oil and rub this into the shaft and grip. Bushmen, strapped for supplies, sometimes use bear oil instead for this purpose, but the drawback to this is that it makes the wood more appetizing to gnawing mice, porcupines, and their brethren.

The paddle is now ready for continued use except that, especially in rocky going, the blade may become distractingly and noisily frayed. After such a trip, therefore, the tip should be evened and tapered off with a keen knife, sandpapered, and then repainted or varnished.

DOUBLE-BLADED PADDLES

As said earlier, the small canoes go much better with a double-bladed paddle. Why it has always been customary to use double paddles on kayaks and single paddles on canoes of the same size is something based only on tradition. For example,

Grumman doesn't even offer a double paddle. The smaller waterline length hasn't the inherent speed characteristics and simply needs the continuous push a double paddle gives. Most common lengths are 8, 8¼, 9, 9½, and 10 ft. Here, again, length depends on beam of boat, length of arms, and the size of the paddler. In one of the tiny one-man canoes one might go as low as 7¼ ft.

ASH, MAPLE OR WHAT?

The veteran canoeist generally comes to own a favorite paddle, just as he also has a pet fishpole, but that often means that he has tried a lot of paddles along the way. What is going to be his choice in the beginning?

One consideration is going to be limberness, the reason the expert is often seen testing the new paddle by angling the tip against one foot and finding out by pressure how much bend there is in the blade, throat, and shaft. This supple, lithe springiness will later be important in absorbing part of the impact that gives a tiring jolt to the hands, wrists, arms, shoulders, back, and even the thighs at the start of each stroke. There's also the distance-covering whip such flexibility can add to the end of each effort.

The ordinary solid, inexpensive spruce paddle is fine for lake work where its lightness is a joy. This softwood's fragility, though, makes it a poorer choice along shallow streams except when it is in the hands of women and careful youngsters whose strength will not ordinarily be enough to break the comparatively brittle shaft. Spruce tips, too, become fuzzy after even a small amount of pushing and prodding.

Ash paddles, though heavier, are commendably rugged and stand up well in gravelly, rocky going. When well made—and it's best to avoid those barrels of sale-priced paddles seen most often in stores where the clerks are more merchants than outdoorsmen, and to concentrate more on the painstakingly crafted paddles of the canoe manufacturers and specialists themselves—ash paddles are satisfactorily limber.

Maple can be a sound compromise, being lighter than ash and stronger than spruce. Maple is a reasonable choice for all-around work, although it is somewhat more apt to warp than ash.

The best laminated paddles combine the advantage of being unusually light to that of handling with extra built-in strength. Some of the most superior paddles are laminated. Beware, though, of bargains. Inferior, cheaply assembled, usually thickly and glossily finished laminated paddles poorly made of scrap woods are on the market, and they will not stand up. These are frequently seen featured at three or four dollars apiece, whereas well-reinforced, reliable laminations cost more, usually between fifteen and twenty dollars.

Paddles with wooden and/or aluminum shafts, the latter sometimes being hollow, and fiberglas blades are the most modern choices for whitewater work and for racing. Both rugged and light, they are easily repaired when damaged.

PADDLE CARE

Paddles are too often used as handy counters upon which fish are cleaned and filleted, then pressed into service as prybars to move logs and even as spades with which to ditch a tent. Actually, it is hard enough on them that they frequently become poles with which a pebbly bottom is navigated and a threatening rock parried. These latter uses cause the blade tip to become frayed, making subsequent strokes blurred and noisy until repairs, as previously considered, can be made.

Warping will be less likely to occur if the damp paddle is kept in the shade as much as possible when not in use. Hardwood paddles are particular offenders in this respect, and especial care must be taken to store these away from the sun. It will be best, too, to take the pressure off of all paddles as by laying them safely off the ground among handy branches where, incidentally, the camper will be less likely to step on one. At the very least, lean them out of the way against a tree, tent, or the canoe itself.

If a paddle does become warped, an Indian remedy is to bury it in moist ground for several days, during which it will usually straighten itself.

Best is to tie the paddles together in pairs, using a short rope that can be draped safely over a branch. This way, too the attractively salt-encrusted grips will be out of the way of hungry porcupines who, in particular, are attracted by such perspiration-enhanced succulencies. When one is camping up above the tree line, it's a sound precaution to bring the paddles into the tent at night, laying them out of the way along the sides.

For winter storage, a convenient provision is a screw eye, in the end of the grip, large enough to encircle a convenient nail, so that the paddle can hang unencumbered.

PADDLING TECHNIQUES

The canoe is in the water. The canoeist, if alone, is kneeling with his paddle, slightly off center, just far enough rear of amidships so that the bow is slightly raised. He is now in position to drive the craft forward, to move it sideways, to propel it backwards, or to spin it in a half-circle so that the stern and bow are suddenly reversed.

Everyone knows how to hold a paddle, one hand on the grip at the end and the other partway down the shaft near the throat where this widens into the blade. The lower hand should be high enough to remain out of the water. This grip is shifted so that the left hand is atop when paddling on the right and the right hand is above when one changes to the left side of the craft.

The blade, of course, is held at right angles to the canoe.

Then reaching forward only as far as is comfortable, bring the blade down into the water and draw it back, sending the canoe ahead. The upper hand continues to push while the lower hand, held at least temporarily extended, serves as a pivot to the lever action. For the utmost impact, both arms should be straight. Many find such practice tiring, however, and let the arms bend naturally as they paddle.

Bring the blade back nearly vertically until it reaches a spot opposite the hip. Do this by pushing with the upper arm, not pulling with the lower arm. Then lift the paddle out with the lower hand, at the same time dropping the upper hand toward the waist so that the blade floats upward and leaves the water.

All important now that the stroke is completed is to relax both arms, an action so restful that it will be possible with a little practice to paddle all day without becoming more than pleasantly tired.

Bring the blade back for another stroke, turning it parallel to the canoe so as to minimize air and any water resistance. Complete all this with the hands and paddle close to, but not scraping, the gunwale or side of the canoe.

All this should be accomplished smoothly and comfortably, with the entire body contributing to the easy and thus enduring power—something that will come naturally with practice.

Basic Stroke

When two individuals are paddling, each works on a different side of the canoe, the canoeist in the stern ordinarily adapting his position to that of the bow paddler. The man in the stern, though, is captain and may direct the bowman with voiced commands, especially when running rapids.

With two paddlers each working from a different side, the direction of the canoe tends to equalize itself. However, the stern paddler usually has to make a special effort to keep it straight. This he does by giving a twist to the blade when it is

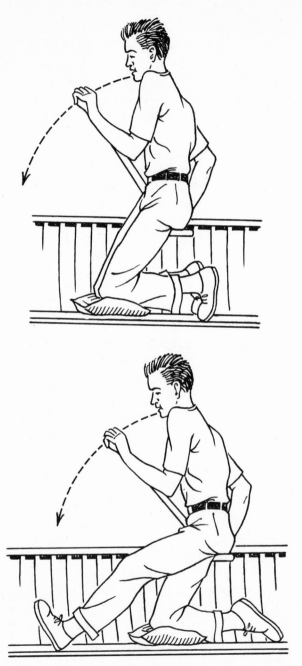

Paddling positions.

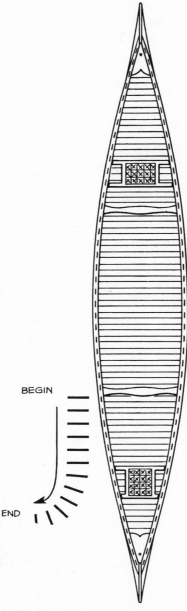

BEGIN

END

The J stroke, a basic steering stroke.

opposite his hip, turning the inside edge of the blade backwards and bringing the entire flatness parallel to the canoe. The paddle thus serves as a rudder, and it is an easy matter to give it a final push to one side or the other to keep the craft on the desired course.

When one is paddling alone, this basic stroke will keep the canoe smoothly and continuously going in the desired direction no matter on which side the canoeist paddles.

Guide Stroke

Again driving the canoe ahead by stroking smoothly parallel to the craft, not being distracted by the curve of the gunwale, the guide stroke varies from the basic stroke in that at the end the blade is brought back feathered underwater—that is, held parallel to the side of the canoe—to a point opposite the hip, where it is withdrawn. Thus, again, the paddle works like a rudder.

This stroke varies among different canoemen, one practice that sacrifices a certain amount of impetus being to hold the blade at a slight angle during the entire sweep, then to make the final correction during the quick upward flip at the end during which the gunwale may serve as the support from which this final bit of pressure is exerted. Both variations, although they take practice at first, can be maintained for hours without undue tiring.

Backing Stroke

The fundamental forward strokes should be mastered first, for it is they that will be used most during the pleasant hour upon hour of canoe travel. When the time comes to halt, slow, or go backwards, merely reverse the cruising stroke.

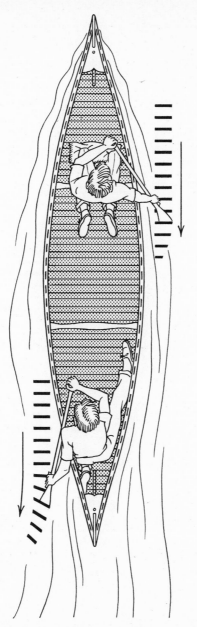

Basic paddling strokes. Correct positions, two canoeists, showing steering twist as executed by stern man.

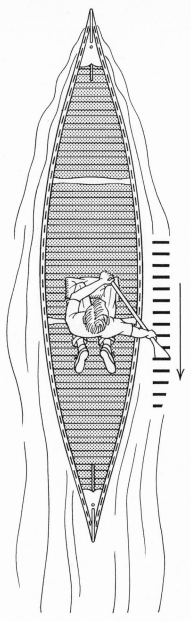

Basic strokes—canoeist paddling alone.

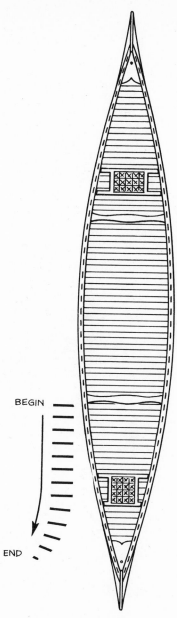

BEGIN

END

The guide stroke.

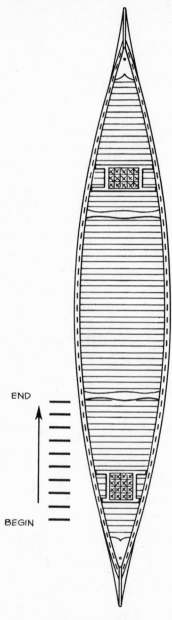

END

BEGIN

The backing stroke.

Jam Stroke

To stop suddenly, plunge the blade vertically into the water at right angles to the canoe. It will be easier to hold it there if one hunches forward over the shaft, pressing this tightly against the side of the canoe with the lower hand.

When two individuals are paddling the one canoe, for the utmost efficiency and balance this jam stroke should be applied simultaneously on signal.

Sweep Strokes

The most difficult stroke to master is the one used for ordinary cruising. This stroke makes good sense throughout, however, whatever variation is used, and skill will come with practice. The other strokes depend on common sense, too, and even the untutored canoeman will find himself practicing most of them without any prior instruction when he needs, for example, to swerve or to turn. Yet it is best to know the best time-saving techniques, for in such a situation as rock-frothing rapids waste motions could be disastrous.

To turn the canoe, swing the paddle like an oar out from and back to the gunwale in a circular sweep. Performed on the left side of the canoe, this will turn the craft to the right. The same thing can be accomplished by a full reverse sweep on the right-hand side. The reverse sweep, of course, starts in back of the canoeist and completes itself in a half circle in front of him.

There are so-called half-sweeps and quarter-sweeps when the turn to be made is less abrupt or where there is more time in which to accomplish it. These are merely shorter sweeps.

When there are two paddlers and each completes a full forward sweep on the same side of the canoe, the craft will swing widely away from the paddles. To pivot a canoe within its own length, the stern paddler should execute a forward sweep and the bowman a reverse sweep on opposite sides.

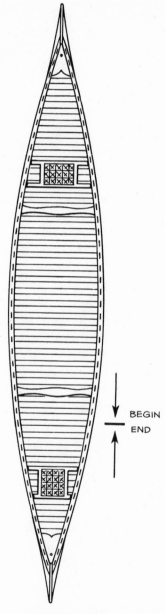

BEGIN

END

The jam stroke.

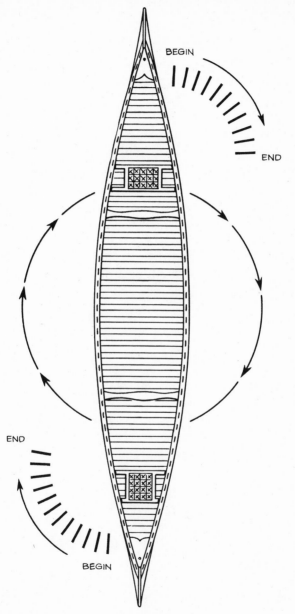

Sweep strokes.

Draw and Push Strokes

The draw stroke, applied to move a canoe broadside, is executed by reaching straight out from the side, with the blade at right angles to the craft, and drawing the paddle straight back towards one. Two paddlers doing this from opposite sides will pivot the canoe sharply.

The push stroke is merely the reverse of this, starting from the paddler's side and pushing straight outward. The same result, of course, can be accomplished with a draw stroke on the opposite side, but there is not always time to shift sides. Again, two canoeists executing a push stroke on opposite sides will rotate the craft.

The push stroke is most effective, abruptly setting over either a bow or a stern depending on which of two paddlers applies it, when the shaft is held against the gunwale and pulled strongly and swiftly inward. Such a drastic stroke, which can break an inferior paddle, is usually reserved for white water.

Throw Stroke

This is a stroke used by the bowman which should be preceded by considerable practice, preferably in safe water at low speeds. Caution is always necessary. If the momentum is too swift, the paddle can be wrenched under the craft and the canoe capsized. Or the paddler may even be yanked into the water or the paddle, if weak, may break.

Throwing the canoe is based on the fact that less momentum is lost on short turns if the bowman at that moment becomes the steersman. The paddle is held perpendicular in the water, close to the gunwale, with the forward edge of the blade straight ahead. If the wrists and arms are strong enough, the bow can be lifted and quickly thrown over to the opposite side, perhaps to evade a rock, by turning the leading edge of the

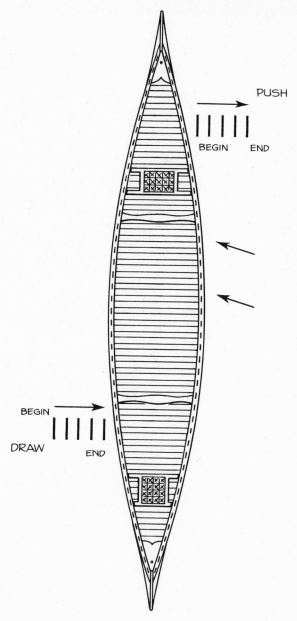

Push and draw strokes.

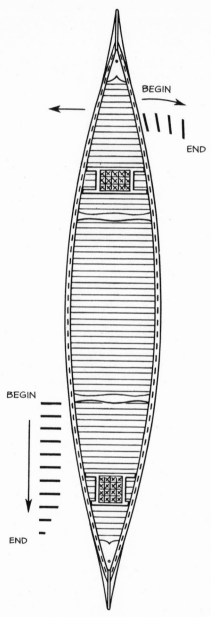

Throw stroke.

blade toward the canoe. The paddle thus acts as a rudder, and it must be held strongly against the resulting wrench.

Practicing these basic strokes so as to become adept with them in all conditions of water and wind makes the skilled, safe, and satisfied canoeist.

CHAPTER THREE

Poling and Outboard Motors

The use of a setting pole is greatly restricted by the kind of water in which it is employed. One works best on a shallow, rocky stream like the sprawling Half Moon of Brunswick's Southwest Miramichi River where, as the stage of water lowers, it becomes increasingly difficult to paddle.

On streams much over four feet deep, such as British Columbia's Peace River, the depth of water is too much. Here except along some of the upper stretches, pulling a pole in and out becomes too cumbersome. On the other hand, on the streams of New England, especially Maine's, poling conditions are just about perfect.

An advantage poling has over paddling is in upstream work where, even with one man, there is nearly continuous power. The only time one loses control of the canoe is for the instant it takes to reset the pole. With two individuals there really can be continuous power.

The reason why poling is not more widely practiced, aside from its being hard work, is probably due to the fact that many streams have soft bottoms. However, one can rig a fork of branches at the end of his regular pole for this sort of going. Too, an opening iron shoe, which closes upon being lifted, is available commercially for the pole point.

POLE SELECTION

One can cut his own pole, although logger's pickpoles, usually of some tough wood such as hickory or ash, may be purchased. When one selects his own pole from along a stream, tamarack or spruce are the two most likely choices. Best by far for the purpose is a sapling, perhaps fire-killed, that has seasoned on the stump.

The pole should be some 12 to 14 feet long, with an average taper of about 1½ inches. The wood is best peeled, then smoothed with a knife. It will be easiest on the hands if left in its natural state, although there are some who like to rub in boiled linseed oil. However, just the oil accumulating from the bare hands will be sufficient.

Iron points, or shoes, are available in the stores, and for best results in rocky channels one should be attached at the larger end. Poles not so equipped do not wear or hold well, although for temporary work one can whittle a point at the thicker butt of the pole, then harden it in the fringes of the campfire for about an hour.

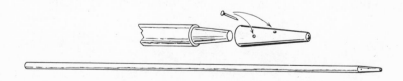

Canoe pole, illustrating poling shoe.

POLING TECHNIQUES

Poling techniques are best learned by practice. Pick a shallow stream, up which the canoe otherwise would perhaps have to be lined or portaged, and pole up it. Or first get the feel of the pole along a shallow lake shore.

Although some handicapped individuals pole from a sitting position, by far the most popular stance is standing in the stern for one man and in both the stern and bow with two canoeists. The canoe should be balanced with the bow riding only a bit higher than the stern. To accomplish this, the lone poler may have to stand near the center of the craft, one leg braced against a thwart. Otherwise, the lead poler should stand slightly off center in the stern with the back leg braced against the seat or rear thwart.

Although, as in paddling, one can pole from both sides, the more powerful thrusts are when the right or master leg is advanced. Stand facing forward with the feet comfortably apart and parallel to the keel. As in riding, there should be give in the knees, which should be partially relaxed, but still springy.

Start in this position by holding the pole with the master hand near the top and with the other hand about a foot and

Poling upstream.

a half below it. Set the pole, close to the canoe, just back of the rear foot. Then, being sure to be well braced and balanced, push. As the canoe moves forward, continue the thrust by climbing the pole hand over hand. When reaching the top of the pole, give a final firm push so as to maintain the momentum while shifting the hands back down toward the middle and resetting the point in the waterway's bottom.

Direction is controlled by push, itself, not by the later resistance of the pole to the water, as might be presumed by paddling techniques. In fact, the pole should be lifted completely clear of the water before being replanted.

Rhythm is important, and this will come with practice. Keep the bow pointed into the current, the canoe parallel to the shore, and in shallow enough water that the bottom can be easily reached. Seek the quietest water where there will be the least pressure from the current. Often, in fact, it will be possible to find backwaters where the water is actually swirling upstream.

Sometimes the pole will be caught between two rocks. Then try to jerk it free. Failing, release the pole before capsizing, and return to it by paddle or by wading.

That's all there is to poling. But it's hard work, although usually not as hard as portaging the canoe and duffle as might have to be done otherwise. Skill comes with practice, and it is encouraging to note that it is usually more easily achieved than mastery of paddling!

THE POLE IN SNUBBING USE

Downstream progress is more a matter of control. Then the pole is used to slow and direct the current-propelled canoe. As in paddling, one still has to select a channel. Again, on strange rivers this is best done from land beforehand.

Although one will probably start the canoe downstream with a soft forward thrust, the rest of the passage will be mostly the hand-over-hand technique in reverse. Try to keep the speed no faster than that of the current itself. Snub the craft frequently by setting the pole ahead and resisting the current. One can even come to a complete stop before setting the canoe over sideways to avoid an obstruction. It is best to keep the canoe parallel to the current.

To snub the canoe, thus slowing or stopping it, reach ahead with the pole to a point about amidship and as close to the gunwale as possible. Upon feeling the pressure, lean into this as much as may be necessary. Several such snubs may be necessary, as in fast white water, to bring the canoe under full control. Practice until mastering this basic technique.

All in all, poling either upstream or down will open new waters to the canoeman.

THE VERSATILE OUTBOARDS

Although the large freight canoes of the Northwest boast outboard motors packing 25 horsepower and more, the average canoe will at the most want no more than a 9½ hp kicker weighing in the vicinity of 70 pounds. No one is going to get a canoe going much above its hull speed, and excess horsepower merely sinks the stern and throws more water about.

The tiny 1½ hp Evinrudes and Johnsons were built for canoes. It's amazing how little effort it takes to push a canoe, although this can be reckoned when one realizes that the craft can be pleasantly paddled all day by one individual. Mercury tests prove that a 3.9 kicker will run an 18-foot Grumman at 11 miles per hour, a 17-footer at 10.8 mph.

Gas Consumption

Before setting out on a canoe trip with an outboard motor, one should have an exact idea of how much distance he can get

Poling and snubbing technique.

out of his gas supply. As the consumption charts show that around 4 to 5 miles per hour is the most efficient canoe speed, one can figure with a fully loaded canoe on getting between 13 and 16 miles per gallon at this pace. However, it is safest to run one's own personal tests beforehand in the particular loaded canoe that is to be used.

In wilderness waters gas caches can be established beforehand along the route by bush pilots and/or Canadian railways.

Outboard Mounts

The side mount has it for comfort. The then conveniently nearby motor can be started and controlled easily. There is no undue fatigue.

However, if one is sliding down a stream and the motor grounds, it can spill the canoe. Likewise, if the motor is pointing at the craft, as it is when starting, and gets going full speed, the sudden push can also capsize the boat.

The stern mount is safer, although it, too, can under certain conditions capsize the boat. One predominant problem is that the sharp end of the usual canoe puts the kicker too far away. It is uncomfortable and a little unsafe to climb back to start the thing, especially with one man, as he loses beam and gains roundness as he goes aft. And while it is possible to rig a handle extension that curves out and forward, so as to come into the hand at a convenient position, this is not an entirely satisfactory arrangement.

The stern mount has it for portaging and for cartopping, as it stays in place when the canoe is lifted. Side mounts, on the other hand, must then be removed. The stern mount allows the aft paddler to utilize both sides for paddling, the side mount only one.

Square Stern

When the canoe is made with a square stern, most of these problems are solved. There is enough room to allow the stern man to get conveniently at the motor. Then, too, since the sharp part of the stern is chopped off, the flatter sections of the hull tend to lift and plane better.

Angle of Attack

A canoe with a square stern and a big motor can lift her snout out of the water, can't stop it, in fact, because there is some planing effect taking place.

In the usual sharp-ended canoe, with either a side or a stern mount, keep the boat on its waterline for best efficiency. With all outboards the shaft of the motor should be at a 90° angle to the water while the boat is in planing or running condition.

Using too heavy a motor on stern gives canoes inefficient cruising characteristics.

Before buying a motor, incidentally, check shaft dimensions against the canoe and mount to be used.

Propeller

It's not as widely known as it should be, but Columbia Propeller, Freeport, N. Y., makes plastic propellers for most small motors that can be driven right through rocks. The plastic—here are those thermal plastics again—bounces right off the obstructions without damage.

As is well known, an aluminum or other metal prop can't hit rocks very hard and very often without severe damage. On wilderness canoe trips with an outboard motor a spare or plastic prop is a must.

CHAPTER FOUR

Canoeing Basics

Most people fear the possibility of capsizing in a canoe, and it can certainly happen. In the normal sitting position, on the seats, the center of gravity is probably higher than in any other boat and, of course, the canoe shape with its roundness can go over easily.

However, if the paddler sits on the bottom as in C1 and C2 canoes and kayaks as well as in the tiniest canoes, the center of gravity will go well below where the center-point of the roll is located and stability will be increased remarkably. This teaches one fast lesson. In any rough water or weather get off the seat and down on the canoe bottom, either sitting or kneeling there. In heavy weather or water, too, it is best to try to center the load and weight, leaving the ends light and free to rise in waves and, if necessary, to spin toward smoother water.

LOW CENTER OF GRAVITY
KNEELING — PADDLING
C-1 IS CENTER OF GRAVITY
C-2 IS THE CENTER OF LATERAL STABILITY
SINCE THE TWO ARE CLOSE IT IS HARD TO CAPSIZE
BOAT.

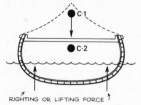

C-1

C-2

RIGHTING OR LIFTING FORCE

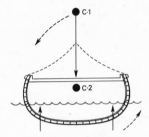

C-1

C-2

HIGH CENTER OF GRAVITY
WHEN MAN SITS ON SEAT
CENTER OF GRAVITY RISES,
DISTANCE OF TURNING
"FULCRUM" IS GREATER.

WITH LONGER "FULCRUM"
IT IS EASIER TO GET
GRAVITY PULL OVERCOMING
CENTER OF STABILITIES
RIGHTING ACTION.

THE LONGER
THIS LINE IS
THE GREATER
IS THE
CAPSIZE
DANGER.

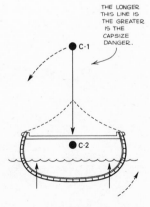

C-1

C-2

CENTER OF GRAVITY
STANDING UP IT'S ALMOST
IMPOSSIBLE TO KEEP CENTER
OF STABILITY IN LINE WITH
CENTER OF GRAVITY.

How the canoe's stability is affected by location of load and center of gravity.

It's important that youths especially should, by predetermined plan and not accident, try swimming with a canoe. This way they can learn about its submerged stability. Too, everyone who uses a canoe should know how to right it and empty it; should become really familiar with it. Learn how to stand up and paddle, even to stand on the gunwales and thus get the fear of tipping over licked once and for all.

All the tricky basics should be learned firsthand, although it should be realized that it's impossible to empty even an unloaded canoe if there is any kind of wave action running. Then as much water will splash in as the canoeist is able to splash out. What experts consider to be the other most fundamental mistakes are these:

1. Greenhorns especially do not realize how cold most of the canoeing waters on this continent are and how very quickly the immersed individual loses the ability to function. This happens all the time to inexperienced canoeists who are in mountain streams in the summer. The day is hot, the stream at 45° or so, and early while shooting a rapids they go overboard, try to swim the rest of the way through while holding to the stern or bow, and become so numb they can't even hold on at the other end. It's been in their minds that because it is July or August the water will be warm.

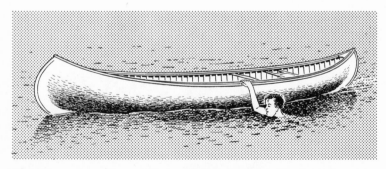

Swimming a canoe. Before doing any extensive canoeing, it's wise to have some practice doing this.

2. Most, too, don't appreciate how frail a canoe can become in big water when the wind starts to blow. If one has a banana boat or a decked canoe, he can last through a hurricane. In an open canoe that's well loaded down, trouble starts when the waves get as little as a foot high. Quickly there is a bailing situation, at the same time all-out attention is needed just to handle the craft.

There is a sea adage that is smart as heck although most people don't fully comprehend it. This is that the time to take all precaution for the safety of the ship is when one *can* take precaution. This is particularly applicable to canoes, their being essentially such fragile crafts. It isn't going to take much in the way of difficulty before one loses the ability to do anything except maybe bail or pray. Canoeists in general shouldn't attempt to cross big water but rather should skirt the edges.

In other words, when canoeing one has to anticipate a potentially bad situation far in advance. By the time the rapids or storm has gripped the craft, it's too late. There's then not much the inexperienced individual can do. Taking precautions means looking well into the future and avoiding risk situations. The canoe is a magnificent craft, but it isn't very forgiving.

RIGHTING A CANOE

To right an immersed canoe that is still floating on its bottom, press down on one gunwale until the craft slowly rolls over. Then, though filled with water, it will stay afloat while the occupants climb back aboard, careful not to roll it under again. They can then sit or kneel on the bottom and paddle ashore, using just the hands if necessary.

Many times, however, the occupants are lurched overboard from a rolling canoe which then rights itself, despite shipping water, before eventually going entirely over. Then, especially in rapids or in wind, it must be regained before it moves beyond reach. If a shore is close, the canoe can be swum back to land.

Otherwise, one swimmer steadies either the bow or the stern with both hands. The other swimmer makes his way amidships, grips the nearer gunwale, brings his body as nearly horizontal as possible in the water at right angles to the canoe, then kicks and pulls himself forward into the canoe, grasping the farther gunwale and bringing his body across both gunwales. From this position, particularly with the second man continuing to steady the canoe, it is a simple matter to roll fully aboard.

There the occupant steadies the canoe to the best of his ability, one hand on each gunwale, while the second swimmer boards in the same manner.

If the canoe has shipped a lot of water, this can be first emptied to a large extent by the swimmers who first press one end as far down as possible so as to empty a large portion of the water, then move amidships and rock the canoe so as to slosh out a good part of the remainder.

THE STORM HAZARD

Canoes can survive in big waves raised by storms. After all, kids are using them like surfboards in ocean breakers. Why

Surviving a capsize in open water, two canoeists.

Step 1—Return to canoe, empty most of water by rocking it.

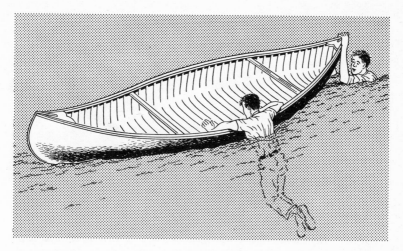

Step 2—While one steadies bow (or stern), other canoeist prepares to scramble aboard.

Step 3—Kicking water to raise his feet and grasping the opposite gunwale, the one canoeist works aboard.

Last step—The canoeist aboard now shifts his weight to stabilize canoe while his partner scrambles aboard.

cruising canoeists get in trouble when storm winds raise big waves is because the bow is not powerful enough to lift the canoe over the waves. The prow sticks into the wave ahead and, of course, the boat is swamped. For this reason, the main heavy-wind-and-wave tactic is evasion; that is, turning and running before the sea.

Since the canoe's speed is allowing the stern to remain in the wave surge a slight time longer than it would otherwise, there is more of a chance for the stern to lift. Also in such a situation, there is the possibilty of stuffing the gear astern, or if necessary in the bow, to create a sort of deck that will throw the water off the sides. Here again, one usually has to antici-pate the need for this. By the time wind or waves get bad enough to demand it, the canoeist likely can't dare to put his weight far enough aft or forward to accomplish it.

The white-water enthusiasts usually use a cover over their open canoes and, in addition, stuff the ends with something such as inflated beach balls for extra flotation.

OVERLOADING

The most common cause of boat accidents is overloading, and this applies in particular to canoes.

Incidentally, on long cruises where heavy loads are nearly unavoidable, especially when one starts out, both weight and bulk can be cut by substituting the modern freeze-dried foods for canned grub, by taking along only the usually adequate tarpaulin or lightweight tent for shelter, and by steadfastly eliminating equipment which is not essential. As with all travel, the more skilled and experienced the canoeist, the lighter his gear.

KNEELING

Seats are for calm water when one is just relaxing and ambling along. Otherwise, both for safety and for efficiency, either sit or kneel on the canoe bottom. When one is using a cushion or something such as a folded, down jacket as a pad for the knees, the kneeling position is preferable and with a little experience can be held for hours without discomfort, particularly if the canoe has a thwart placed so that the paddler can rest his rear against it.

Birch-bark and other early Indian canoes, including those made with hides, had no seats, these being a later American paleface innovation now widely adopted by the Canadians. Previously, many of the canoes north of the border used to have special low thwarts or crossbars against which the canoeman could lean, making him an almost solid part of the boat and assuring full use of the arm, neck, shoulder, back, and thigh muscles. One can get much the same effect by kneeling comfortably in front of the modern seat, bow and stern.

When one is alone in an otherwise empty canoe, he should balance the craft so that the bow is only slightly higher than the stern by kneeling slightly behind the center thwart or, especially if firmer balance is needed as in rough seas or in a race, by kneeling on one knee with the other leg secured over this center thwart. In both instances, kneel a bit off-center instead of directly over the keel, so that the canoe will ride slightly on the paddling side, making propulsion easier. As experience is gained, comfort and techniques will improve.

STANDING

The best way when afloat to make a quick survey of the rapids one is about to shoot is by standing. This is also the most satisfactory procedure for spotting obstructions in shallow water. Canoe fishermen can get added distance and accuracy in their casts if they are erect. Too, standing in a canoe is almost a necessity when one is poling. For enchanting, relaxing pleasure while paddling along an intriguingly placid shore, try it standing.

In other words, the often-repeated axiom that one should never stand in a canoe is heard only from individuals not experienced with the craft.

CHANGING POSITION

The stern paddler and the bowman can change positions afloat if proper deference is paid to balance, but why bother? The usual canoe paddles almost equally well in either direction. All that's necessary for a shift in position, in other words, is just to face about. In fact, the best rule is never change places in a floating canoe.

BOARDING

The same sort of overcaution as to not standing is seen among tyros when it comes to boarding the canoe, and this sometimes makes for a loss of balance. Be careful, yes, but get aboard with more confidence than preciseness. In other words, with a loaded canoe especially, it is not necessary to make a long step directly over the keel, then to ease cautiously into position.

First of all, the canoe should be completely afloat. Then the stern man, being the captain, steadies it while any passengers step aboard and settle themselves on the floor, followed by the bowman. The latter then takes on the job of steadying, perhaps holding to a wharf or bank or shoving his paddle firmly against the bottom while the stern man gets into position.

When landing, the succession is reversed. The stern paddler gets the canoe into position, then steps out, perhaps into the water, and holds the craft for the bowman to disembark. Both hold the canoe while the passenger gets off.

Again, to stress the point, the canoe should be afloat before it is boarded. When the canoe is drawn up on shore with most of the boat in the water, for example, it is most capsizable. This unsteadiness is increased by anyone's sitting on the seat rather than standing on the floor. The reason is the same as when tending that aft outboard. One becomes balanced on the round part of the bottom. The flat section of the bottom that is

Procedure for boarding canoe at dock; use reverse technique for disembarking at dock.

in the water is severely reduced, and the occupant is, in effect, trying to balance himself on the bottom half of a round ball.

Getting into canoes on the beach, half in and half out with the middle weight not supported as is all too common, is a good way to damage them, especially in the case of wood and canvas boats. The aluminum and plastic canoes are more durable.

Incidentally, when embarking from sand or gravel, it will protect the finish of the canoe if one first washes the soles of his shoes before making that last step from land.

NEEDED—A PAINTER

Every canoe should have a painter, a short tethering rope about 25 feet long, fastened to the prow. When the canoe goes ashore, this painter should be tied to something solid such as a rock or tree. Otherwise, a rise of water might very well float the craft loose, or a gust of wind might blow it adrift. Canoes are so light, especially in relation to their broad sail-like surfaces, that this danger is a very real one, and more than one canoeist has suddenly looked over his campfire to find himself marooned.

LANDING

It is unduly rough on both the paint and the structure of a canoe bottom to beach it prow first, as is commonly done on sand and even gravel. Instead, whether landing at a beach or a pier, come directly in, slowly enough that at the last moment the stern man swings the canoe to his master side, usually the right, and the bowman backs up the action, bringing the craft in parallel. Then be ready to step off into shallow water if necessary, or perhaps to a ledge or rock, with the canoe still fully afloat.

Approach procedure when not landing and disembarking from a canoe on sandy or gravel shoreline.

Bow man disembarks first while stern paddler holds canoe steady. Same procedure can be used for boarding canoe from a shoreline.

The exception is the landing made in heavy weather, particularly when it is not possible to reach quiet water. Again, come in directly, at right angles to the rock shelf, for instance. Instead of then trying to come around parallel, the stern man steps off into the water, preferably before any contact is made. He then steadies the canoe while the bowman steps into the water. Both steady the boat while any passenger disembarks. Then both move on opposite sides to the middle of the craft, there grasping the gunwales and half-lifting and half-floating the craft, move it in beyond the turbulence.

Illustrating method of disembarking (or boarding) canoe when it is not landed on gravel or sandy shoreline.

Incidentally, clean canoes are less apt to attract hungry bears and porcupines. This is especially important if the cruisers have been successfully hunting or fishing. Porcupines are no threats to aluminum and plastic craft, if the paddles are kept well out of their reach, but a hungry bear could well stave in a side.

LOADING

Ideally, the canoe should be in the water when loaded, but practically it can be partially beached, yet not so much that it will not be easy to lift its beached end and ease this back into the water.

If the load is not too bulky, a stratagem to keep it drier will be to lay first either several poles or a matting of evergreen boughs on the bottom. Such a practice also tends to make bailing easier.

The heavier items go down first, everything being balanced

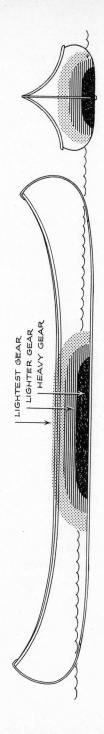

LIGHTEST GEAR
LIGHTER GEAR
HEAVY GEAR

Loading gear into canoe—two-man outfit.

so that the canoe will lie evenly in the water with the bow slightly higher than the stern. The exceptions to this last is that an evenly trimmed canoe proceeds best downwind on lakes, while a lighter stern makes for increased maneuverability in rapids. If at all possible, when the crew and duffle are all aboard there should be at least six inches of freeboard—the distance between the top of the lowest gunwale and the water.

STREAMSIDE REPAIRING

One should always carry one of the small, inexpensive repair kits designed for his particular canoe. With one of these, minor streamside repairs are easy. Otherwise, improvisations may become necessary, limited only by the materials at hand and by one's ingenuity. For example, in a pinch a canvas canoe can be patched with a piece of duffle bag or clothing, held on by melted or chewed conifer pitch in which ideally a bit of bacon grease and charwood from the campfire has been mixed. Small holes, too, can be patched with chewing gum, manufactured or wild, or with plain electrician's tape, preferably plastic.

The best way to handle a small tear, perhaps triangular, is first to lift the surrounding canvas very carefully with the point of a knife. Then cut a piece of canvas large enough to overlap the original injury substantially, coat it on one side with the adhesive in the purchased or improvised repair kit, slip it underneath with the glue upward, and press everything down firmly with anything flat, perhaps with the added weight of a rock. That part of the canoe should first have been allowed to dry as much as possible, of course.

When everything is set, cut a rounded, somewhat larger piece of fabric from the emergency roll, spread adhesive both on the damaged portion of the canoe and on one side of the patch, and then cover the place with the second patch. Keep

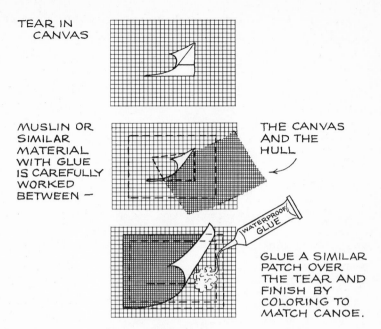

TEAR IN CANVAS

MUSLIN OR SIMILAR MATERIAL WITH GLUE IS CAREFULLY WORKED BETWEEN —

THE CANVAS AND THE HULL

WATERPROOF GLUE

GLUE A SIMILAR PATCH OVER THE TEAR AND FINISH BY COLORING TO MATCH CANOE.

Repair method—wood/canvas canoe.

under pressure until dry and except in appearance, the canoe will be as good as new.

When the tear is more than a foot long, it will be a sound idea to stitch the first patch to the original canvas with a needle and heavy thread before applying the second patch.

Broken ribs present more of a problem, and this is where ingenuity will come into play. One possibility, for example, will be to split a green hardwood sapling, one with about a two-inch diameter, bend it into rib shape with the flat side on the outside, wedge it into position, and lash each end to a gunwale.

Another maneuver will be to set a substantial flattened block against the readjusted injury on the inside of the canoe, then to wedge it there with an improvised rib like the one

mentioned above or with a short upright between the canoe
bottom and a thwart to which it is lashed. In both cases, the
canvas is then waterproofed by one of the methods previously
considered.

Broken ribs or frames can also be pressed gently back into
position, then laced with copper wire. Lacing cut from the
root bark of one of the wild cherry trees will work, as will
small boiled spruce roots. For a particularly tight job use wet
rawhide lacing, which will shrink upon drying.

ALUMINUM STREAMSIDE REPAIRING

Marred aluminum canoes should have all metal surfaces flattened out as much as possible. At the point of the injury that
is to be repaired, the metal on both sides should be roughed.
Heavy sanding is all right, but in a pinch one can do the
roughening with a knife tip. Then the tear or puncture is
covered with fiberglas and saturated with epoxy resin. Polyester resin? This will not only raise the paint, but it does not
stick to metal or anything as well as the recommended epoxy.
The area, which of course should have been dry to start with,
should harden in a couple of hours. Then if a patch is a big
one, several layers should be added. Incidentally, extend the
fiberglas an inch out from the cut.

A difficulty streamside arises when the tear is a big one,
whereupon the area should be backed with something such as
paper, cloth, birch bark, or cardboard to hold the resin in
place while drying. Best is cellophane because the resin, not
sticking to this, will then not be absorbed by it. Generally,
after the initial coat, hardening, has been absorbed to fill the
holes in the cloth or paper backing, the next coat won't drip
away.

A kit for emergency repairs should include a square yard of
10-ounce cloth (the so-called standard weight), a pint of

epoxy with hardener, and a knife for cutting the cloth and spreading the resin.

PERMANENT ALUMINUM REPAIRS

If the tear or puncture is small, the just mentioned method will probably last well enough. Many a damaged aluminum canoe that has been repaired in this fashion continues to be waterproof for years. But if the tear is large and structural strength has been lost, or if the patch remains under stress, more permanent repairs should be undertaken when one is back home.

Necessary will be some good aluminum. Write to the manufacturer for this, find a local supply house, or go to a nearby airport where they repair aluminum planes. If a workman skillful enough to weld the spot is available, fine. Welding is best. Otherwise, the traditional aluminum repair method must be resorted to.

Flatten the tear. Cut an aluminum patch to cover, one that will extend an inch beyond the injury all around. Now drill for rivets every two inches around the damage. Rivet with aluminum rivets after spreading a non-hardening seam compound. Again, the difficulty is finding adequate materials. Probably a boat dealer won't have any idea where to secure these. Someone at one's local airport probably will.

FIBERGLAS REPAIRS

Fiberglas is liable to shatter, so it is fortunate that permanent repairs can be made streamside. First, dish out the break or puncture in concave fashion using a wood rasp.

Lay the first layer of 10-ounce glass cloth in the depression. Polyester can be used as the adhesive, as it sticks well to glass and paint is removed by the rasping. Again, some care must be exercised that the resin doesn't seep away, and this is prevented by backing. After the concavity is built up, cut one or more patches in ever-increasing sizes. Two patches is a minimum, but no more than three are needed. The resin soaks more evenly after the first patch.

Any break on the outside or inside can be easily smoothed by chopping glass into a dust and adding resin to make a putty. The only tool needed is a rasp, and actually a knife can be substituted. Resin can be applied with a knife, too. Just pour it on and smooth into place. If one makes a rough repair at streamside, it can be smoothed later with a disc sander and rough sandpaper. Finish off with fine sandpaper. The area can then be painted if the color can be matched, or the entire canoe can be brightened with a fresh coat.

As is evident, fiberglas can be repaired by anyone who can remember not to forget the hardener, a common mistake. Just slurp it on and grind off the crudity later.

RESTORING CANOES REALLY BUSTED!

No aluminum or fiberglas canoe should be abandoned. It happens all the time that canoes are horseshoed around rocks in fast water. But aluminum can be pounded out, although it may be a tedious job, then welded. Fiberglas that is snapped amidships by the same hazard can be fixed at the break as has been suggested. Then stiffening pieces of cloth, running lengthwise, will restore the structural strength.

For small tears and punctures, some of the plastic putties can go right on over the hole. These harden like iron, one of the best of them being Marine-Tex. Just spread a layer, set a patch of glass cloth in it while it is still soft, then smooth a layer of putty on top. This will stop a .22 bullet after it sets. Almost any auto body shop can easily fix a glass canoe, by the way.

PADDLE REPAIR

A cracked paddle can often be successfully reglued with the two-part epoxy adhesive. Then clamp, as with an elastic band

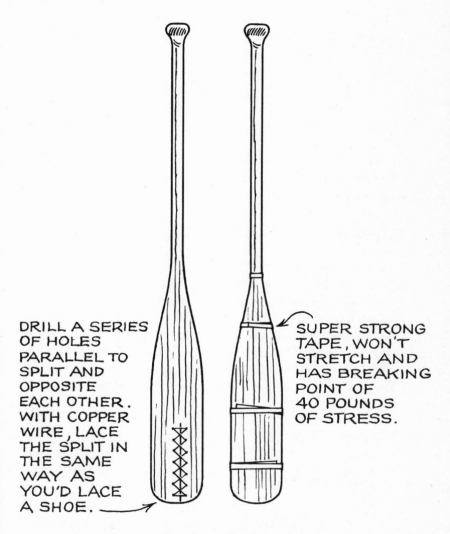

DRILL A SERIES
OF HOLES
PARALLEL TO
SPLIT AND
OPPOSITE
EACH OTHER.
WITH COPPER
WIRE, LACE
THE SPLIT IN
THE SAME
WAY AS
YOU'D LACE
A SHOE.

SUPER STRONG
TAPE, WON'T
STRETCH AND
HAS BREAKING
POINT OF
40 POUNDS
OF STRESS.

Repairing a split paddle.

cut from an innertube, or lash until the glue has set. To back up the new joining, some like to add a fabric-and-glue patch on each side, a process that is sometimes used alone.

For a repair job that will likely be stronger and longer-lasting than the paddle itself, as when the sun cracks a wet hardwood blade, drill a line of tiny holes about ½-inch apart and the same distance back from the break on each side of the split. Then lace with fine copper wire from the repair kit.

Split shafts can be wound with fishline, adhesive tape, or with wet rawhide lacing that will tighten upon drying. If the injury is severe, thin wooden splints—preferably from a tree or sapling that has died on the stump—can be added for reinforcement.

In any event, a spare paddle should always be at hand, probably shoved under the lashings of the load where it can be grabbed in an instant.

CANOE CARE AND STORAGE

The aluminum and plastic boats need little care. Plastics can be waxed each year, and they'll retain their gel coat better. Sanding, revarnishing, and repainting are apt to become an-nual spring chores with the canvas and wood craft.

The best place to store a boat is on a rack. More canoes, especially in the crowded places, are stored in garages than in any other single place. The owner runs his car in and lashes the canoe to the beams where it remains until the next time.

CHAPTER FIVE

Lake Cruising

The best way to deal with lake crossings is to avoid them whenever at all practical. Instead, skirt the shores. This will take more time, but it is far less dangerous, especially as a heavily loaded canoe has little freeboard and only a small amount of lift. Besides, it is far more interesting to paddle, sail, or cruise along the edge of the always varying land.

If one day a sudden shift in the weather does catch the canoeist in the open, he should get everything as low as possible and run at a slight angle to the waves. But more of this later.

SHIPPING WATER

Taking in water, a common occurrence in canoe travel everywhere, is not dangerous so long as it can be bailed out faster than it is coming in. This suggests that a bare minimum procedure before setting out across any open water will be to get bailing cans ready for all crew members and to trim the canoe so the moisture will run to a spot where it can be tossed overboard.

Insofar as ballast is concerned, in any kind of a storm all weight in the boat should be on the canoe bottom to increase stability. This will be particularly true if it suddenly becomes necessary to run sideways to wind and waves. A savage gust could then conceivably capsize the boat just from its force on the seated paddlers.

Such sideways paddling is when quarts of water will slop aboard and the bailing can will come robustly into play. A heavily laden canoe has little freeboard, one that is ordinarily measured in no more than scant inches. The canoe's

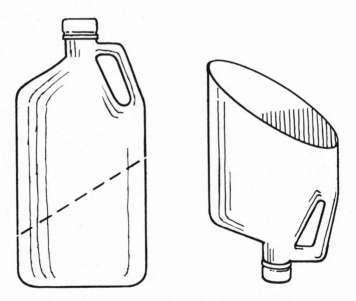

Bailing scoops are easy to improvise from empty plastic containers which would otherwise be discarded after household use.

cigar shape, so fine for carrying and for easy paddling, isn't much for seaworthiness, certainly not when loaded. This shape does many things magnificently, but it does not bounce up waves worth a hoot and, since the usual canoe is wide open, water sometimes comes aboard in generous quantities.

While the canoe rates first place in portability, it lags well down the line in seaworthiness, a fact that most individuals do not understand. A flat-bottomed cartopper, for example, which may not weigh a great deal more, is ten times more capable in stormy weather because it has at least twice as much beam as a canoe to lift it to waves. Furthermore, people don't normally figure on loading other boats down below six inches of freeboard, the way canoes are often laden.

Native fishermen continually overload canoes in this fashion. But the beginning canoeist should see these natives bail! They use wooden dustpanlike scoops for the most part, and when they bail the water comes out in a steady, continuous stream, almost as if someone had turned on a hose. They know that the canoe itself can not keep the water out and that this function is up to them.

STORM TECHNIQUES

If one has to drive into big seas, it is usually wisest not to hit them straight on. Instead, meet them at a slight angle so that more of the bow, and consequently more lifting surface, is presented to the wave. Then as the canoe rises it will kind of roll over the wave, tilting away from it at first, then leaning toward the wave's direction as the surge of water passes underneath.

This is the time for short, swift strokes. When there are two paddlers, these strokes need not even be in rhythm. In fact, alternate efforts may even keep the canoe on a more stable course. With heavy gusts catching the bow, both may paddle on the quieter side to balance the wind pressure.

When trying to proceed against big seas, paddle at a slight angle to them, not directly into them.

One thing to avoid, a mistake that's far too easy to make when the travelers are heading for a lee shore, is not to force the canoe too hard against incoming combers. This way it may nose-dive into each wave, shipping too much water. Let the bow lift. Then keep the canoe under firm control once it is balanced on the crest, as the tendency will be for it to swerve downwind into the forward trough with the resultant risk of capsizing. The stern man should power the craft straight ahead. The bowman should paddle into the wind.

Once the balance of the canoe slides over the crest, the stern in turn will lift. Then too much paddle will plunge the bow into the next wave instead of over it. In such a situation, the first objective will be to lift over each wave, glide through its crest, and then descend the farther side without shipping more water than one has time to handle. The second objective will be to make headway.

If possible, practice beforehand near a safe shore wearing life jackets and preferably bathing suits. The bowman in particular is important in such a situation, where a major problem will be to lift the bow over each oncoming surge of water.

At the decisive instant, the bowman can help by actually lifting himself on flexed thighs, at the same time thrusting downward into the wave with the flat of his paddle. All this must be accomplished so smoothly that the canoe is not veered and so that he'll be once more in paddling position as soon as the canoe glides over the top of the wave.

Suppose the paddler is alone? Then, kneeling as far amidships as will be necessary to balance the craft, he should drive the canoe into wind and waves at such an angle that he can do all his paddling on the lee side. The wind pressure will then bear more strongly on the stern, itself assisting the canoe to remain on course.

RUNNING BEFORE THE WIND

Perhaps one day the canoe will be a lot nearer the shore opposite to that from which a sudden squall blows. The lake is miles wide. The safest course will be to run downwind.

In such high seas the major problem will be to keep from broaching. Too much paddling, added to the impetus of the

When a canoeist is alone and compelled to paddle against wind and wave he drives the canoe at an angle to the waves and does his paddling on the lee side.

storm, will tend to drive the canoe downward into troughs. Instead, ride a wave as long as possible. Then, using the stern paddle as a rudder, keep the canoe straight as it settles stern-first into the following trough and is gripped by the next comber. This will likely take every last ounce of the canoeist's strength, especially when he is beginning to tire. The bowman can help at each such decisive instant by holding the front of the canoe downwind.

When the canoeist knows beforehand that he is going to run downwind in heavy seas, he can rig a stabilizing sea anchor by hanging a water pail to the end of about a 25-foot-long rope fixed to the center of the stern gunwale. Thrown overboard, this will pull the stern into the wind and hold it there. Then steerage, while taking full advantage of the headway afforded by the wind and waves themselves, will be far easier.

When running before strong wind and following seas a water bucket can be towed as an improvised sea anchor to make steerage easier.

This does not mean that such a passage should be attempted except in an emergency. It will be far more satisfactory, and an experience that will thereafter reign high among one's adventures, to camp and let the wind blow itself out. Gales frequently quiet at dawn and again at dusk, and it may be possible at either of these times to complete a short passage. On other occasions one may have to stay camped on a sheltering island for the better part of a week.

FLOTATION PROVISIONS FOR SAFETY

The good canoes will have plenty of built-in flotation, but off-brand boats should be inspected with a callous eye. Wood and canvas craft, of course, will not sink because of the inherent buoyancy of the wood; aluminum and fiberglas because of flotation substances or chambers built in their hulls.

Many individuals, when canoeing on streams, lash their gear into the canoe so that if they spill, everything isn't lost. This should not be done in an open-water situation when the weight of the outfit would sink the boat. Maybe lash essentials like food and an axe, but let the motor, sleeping gear, fishing tackle and such go rather than risk having the boat sink.

A swamped canoe is a thousand times better than no canoe at all, however. For one thing, it can be spotted much more easily than a floating individual, and it is immediately recognized as being in trouble. Sitting in a swamped boat gets the person mostly out of the water. The boat offers some sense of security and tends to inhibit panic.

As in all boating, no one should ever be allowed to leave the swamped canoe and hit out for the shore even though land may seem absurdly close. The procedure is to swim the canoe toward shore.

There is another technique of loading a canoe, especially for river work, that has many times proved itself in emergencies and which is practiced by many professional woodsmen. This is to pack the heavy objects like canned food unsecured on the bottom of the canoe; first, it should be well noted, scratching or otherwise permanently marking the contents of each can on its lid. Then spread a tarpaulin open over these. In this, pack the essentials such as extra clothing, a nucleus of the lighter foods such as bacon, eggs and tea, and so on, topping all this with the highly buoyant sleeping bags.

Bring the edges of the tarpaulin up and enclose these necessities in their own bundle, not fastening this to the canoe in

The swamped canoe will still stay enough afloat to support one or more canoeists until help arrives or until the craft drifts to shore or shallows, but very cold water can still spell trouble if the period of immersion is too long.

any way. Stick an axe in the lashings where it can be easily reached without unpacking, as for clearing a portage. The heavy gun, as when one is hunting for trophies or meat, can be tied to the canoe, itself, with a long line from a thwart to loop through the trigger guard. Fishing gear, when it's all in one place, can likewise be tied to the canoe.

Then in case of trouble, as when a canoe is caught amid-ships by a rock that holds it broadside to the current which can then break it in two, the essentials will float separately and can be retrieved by following the shore downstream. It is usually possible, too, to reach the wreckage long enough to retrieve a single item such as a rifle. Incidentally, canoeists should make sure that their telescopic sights are waterproof.

LIFE JACKETS

Life preservers—that is, separate and usually detached units for keeping an individual afloat—are the unhandiest sort of buoyant devices to have on a canoe. But they are the least that should be aboard the craft at all times. Generally they are seen in the form of cushions. The cushioning characteristic is functional in a canoe, if only for kneeling on when paddling, but the trouble from the life-preserver aspect is that they're prone to become hopelessly flattened by daily use. Too, in rapids especially, a cushion is apt to bob out of reach if the canoe is capsized.

Any canoeist venturing into the excitement of white water,

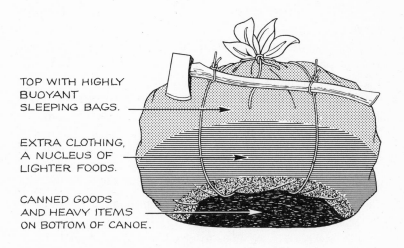

TOP WITH HIGHLY BUOYANT SLEEPING BAGS.

EXTRA CLOTHING, A NUCLEUS OF LIGHTER FOODS.

CANNED GOODS AND HEAVY ITEMS ON BOTTOM OF CANOE.

Enclosing the equipment load with a tarpaulin.

boating on cold water, or crossing big water should wear a preserver. There are plenty of boat coats and flotation jackets available today. There are inflatable vests. There are wrist preservers that inflate at a touch. And, of course, there are the familiar orange collar preservers that go over the neck and extend down the front. Non-swimmers should be required to wear at least one of these in any risk-type situation.

Even when one is canoeing with a group, preservers should be worn in deference to the long-established survival rule: hope for the best but prepare for the worst. By the time one canoe gets in trouble from storm or rapids, the others will be having similar difficulties that may make rescue impossible or at the very least delayed.

Even an inflated beach ball is better than nothing to hang on to. Some wilderness canoeists make a practice of having their rolled, usually highly buoyant sleeping bags where they can be grabbed in an emergency. Most cruise rental enterprises require that the orange collar preservers be worn. Too, plenty of canoe clubs composed of really experienced individuals have the same requirement.

Probably the worse kind of preserver in common use is the water skier's collar worn at the waist. Obviously, this won't hold an unconscious individual's head up, and in fact one has to be a pretty good swimmer to keep his head up with such a device even under the best conditions.

Good, comfortable preservers, made to be worn while one is still unhampered, are usually required on racing sailboats. These ribbed or slab-foam jackets cost more than the under-five-dollar cushion type and employ the new polyvinyl chloride and/or polyethylene closed-celled foam instead of the perishable kapok which eventually powders under use. Incidentally, balsa wood and cork have both been banned as buoyant materials in life vests.

It is always a good idea to check one's personal flotation device to make sure it is adequate, doing this in shallow water.

Make sure that arms and legs are below the surface and relaxed. Pull the knees up to a sitting position to keep from
standing on the bottom. Then note the buoyant characteristics
of the lifesaver.

The flotation device one depends upon on a canoe trip
should have sufficient buoyancy to keep both neck and head
out of water. It should be both comfortable and easy to don
and remove, at the same time allowing freedom of movement
in and out of water. It should not have a tendency to turn and
press the wearer in a face-down position. It should have the
characteristics of drying quickly and easily after leaving the
water.

Especially for use in open water, it is best when highly
visible. It should be resistant to aging, weathering, extreme
changes in temperature, and to oil products. Its condition
should remain evident through visual inspection. Such a personal flotation device should be bought to fit the individual
and to be worn only by him, thus establishing both confidence
and a sense of safety.

Do swimmers need to be concerned with lifesaving devices?
The answer lies in the fact that the greatest number of drown-
ings have taken place among good swimmers.

When all is said and done about the life preserver, the most
important consideration is that the thing be there when it's
needed.

SUBNORMAL BODY TEMPERATURE—
A DEADLY HAZARD

A personal flotation device that will float the individual to start
with can be expected to sustain him for an indefinite period.
However, water temperature and exposure will likely have the
first detrimental effects and these are measured in minutes and
hours.

Immersion hypothermia, subnormal body temperature, in-

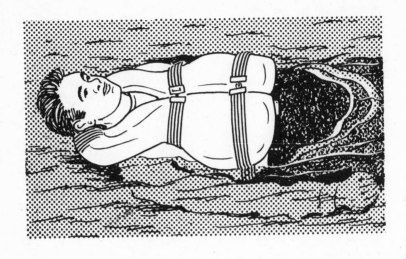

Flotation pieces for personal safety should be fully capable of supporting the canoeist so that his head and neck will be out of water.

volves the loss of body heat to the water. It is assumed that an individual will succumb if his normal temperature, about 98.6°, falls as much as twenty degrees. In waters warmer than 70°, heat production may be expected to keep pace with heat loss. Then fatigue, leading to ultimate exhaustion, is the limiting factor.

The following chart shows the effect of exposure:

Water Temperature (°F)	Unconsciousness or Exhaustion	Expected Survival Time
32.5°	Under 15 min.	Under 15-45 min.
32.5°-40°	15-30 min.	30-90 min.
40°-50°	30-60 min.	1-3 hr.
50°-60°	1-2 hr.	1-6 hr.
60°-70°	2-7 hr.	2-40 hr.
70°-80°	3-12 hr.	3-indef.
80° Plus	Indef.	Indef.

PASSENGER WEIGHT AND BALANCE

Canoe passengers can pose problems if they get excited and shift their weight at exactly the wrong time. For this reason their weight should be on the canoe bottom, not on a seat or sitting on gear. They should be positioned along with the duffle so that the craft lies evenly in the water, the bow probably a bit higher than the stern. Passengers never paddle, although they may exchange chores with the stern or bowman.

SAILS AND THE CANOE

A small sail is a great asset on lake cruises when down-wind work can be expected. The Indians cut small trees and held them aloft. This works!

A sail goes in the bow, while the canoeist in the stern steers with his paddle. It isn't necessary to get fancy, although

Gunter and lateen sails, mounted on a single mast and stepped in a special thwart or mount on some canoes, allow tremendous speeds which, in turn, call for the most skilled seamanship. For extensive sailing, leeboards, sail, mast, etc. are supplied in commercial auxiliary sailing kits.

One can get by very well on the lakes of the United States and Canada with an otherwise ground cloth that has been rigged with grommets so that it can be lashed to a sapling. This in turn is lashed to another sapling and tied to a forward thwart to make a jury-rigged square sail. With a simple rig like this the canoe can be sailed downwind at an angle of 45° or so of the wind.

Using an improvised sail. Even a small sail improvised from a ground cloth can save much paddling. To lessen the sail's adverse effect on canoe stability it should be mounted so its bottom edge barely clears the gunwales (use a mast no longer than necessary) and mast and boom material, while it must be strong enough, could likely also be of smaller pieces than suggested here.

While canoe sailing has interesting possibilities, it usually involves more open water canoeing than would be wise for the inexperienced to undertake and its applications in ordinary wilderness cruising are limited.

THE WEATHER HAZARD

It is *wind* that is the danger. Rain, though perhaps disagreeable, isn't dangerous. Squalls are very hazardous. The worst are cold fronts that appear as a long black line. But a thunderstorm can generate winds up to about 60 miles per hour. Getting caught on open water in one is too often an invitation to the undertakers.

High steady winds create big waves. Often in lakes, though, especially the island-studded Canadian lakes, one can find a lee shore and make progress.

Many of the reservoir lakes in the Southwest hold a danger in that the desert heat creates thermals which are channeled by the hills and manifest themselves as savage wind gusts. These don't last long and usually don't build up big waves. But they may hit the canoe at 90 mph. If the canoeist sees one coming—noting the oncoming streaks on the water—he should get his weight down as low as possible and head into it.

Lightning is an overrated danger, only 600 in this country being killed by it annually. But the sound and sight of the bolts are often terrifying. One is much safer then on land than on water. If caught in a thunderstorm, the best procedure will be to take the canoe ashore in a group of trees all about the same height. Avoid heights, as well as single trees in the open. Turning the canoe over and getting under it will give shelter as well as an increased feeling of security.

CHAPTER SIX

River Running

Supreme thrills await the canoeist who leaves smooth water behind and heads his boat into white-water rapids. Suddenly the current quickens. The canoe bucks its way past rocks that roar with the noise of water breaking over and around them, plows through great frothy walls of the stuff, and finally shoots through into the clear. River-running presents moments fraught with exhilaration and excitement. It is also the most dangerous of all forms of canoeing. Each year attractive white-water stretches reach out to claim their toll in broken up canoes and loss of lives—lives lost needlessly, sacrificed on the twin altars of ignorance and foolhardiness.

RESPECT WHITE WATER

The fact is, the novice canoeist should approach any white water worthy of the name with the same respect he would allot to a climb up a sheer rock wall. Yet the rock wall is somewhat self-regulatory. Hard effort, crumbling footholds, and the dizzy look down soon put the novice mountain climber in full awareness of the situation.

The budding but bungling white-water canoeist can expect no such built-in protection. Once he is committed, escape from a white-water nightmare is open only to experts. The amateur soon loses all control over his boat. The river takes charge, throwing its vast armament of rocks, ledges, waterfalls, and fallen trees with impersonal fury at its terrified and helpless victim. The result is dismally predictable and at best a sunken canoe, equipment scattered and ruined, and occupants soaked, sodden, bruised, and chastened.

At the worst, disaster awaits. Even on sunny summer days, river waters run cold. Its effect has been discussed. All canoeists should get out of the ice-cold deep water as soon as possible, even sacrificing the canoe if need be. Even when he is out of the water, be wary of a soaked victim's assurances that he is all right. His strength is being sapped faster than he realizes. No time must be spared in getting him into dry clothes. If anyone must enter cold water, let him strip so that he can come back and let the dry clothes warm him.

Just as ignorance masks the danger of cold water, it fails to calculate the staggering forces of hydraulics. Engineers estimate the thrust of an average-sized canoe immersed crossways in a 10-mile-an-hour current as more than *three tons!* Even when one is standing thigh-deep in such current, a weight of more than 300 pounds forces itself against the wader's legs. (Rapids faster than 10 mph do exist, but they are rare.)

The much more frequent river-killer is all the more sinister because it strikes without warning and instantaneously. A dancing rapids is attempted. The canoe grounds on a rock, swings sideways, capsizes. Several occupants are swept downstream, getting nothing but a wetting for their pains. Another is not so lucky. He is spilled ahead of the canoe which the current forces against a rock, pinning the individual. If his head is above water, there is a chance for life. If not, picture the situation.

Those who know of the mishap, being swept downstream themselves, may not even notice the victim's absence until too late. If they do, fighting their way to shore and back upstream may take too long. Boats following may or may not see what has occurred, and if they do, they are probably fighting for survival themselves. Or—the pinned person may be in an unapproachable area.

It is a deadly web of coincidental but interconnected circumstances—so much so that canoe clubs will send their best team down bad stretches to take post on rocks or ashore so accidents can be spotted, reported, and rescue efforts instituted at once.

None of this has to be, of course. Skill, equipment, training and experience enable members of white-water canoe clubs to conquer the toughest rapids in the country with ease and in complete safety. The novice approaches this as all else in stages, a step at a time, carefully learning to balance the challenge of the singing waters with his own mastery over them.

READING THE RIVER

A white-water rapids is like a sparkling and attractive, yet simple-headed young girl. She is always changing, but her frailties and strengths are easy to distinguish. One can even tell the mood of this charmer by the tone of her voice. Does she sing a lilting soprano? Expect the rapids to be delicate and rippling. Is her tone more of a deep-throated roar? The rapids-runner can expect more powerful problems. When the lady gets angry, she bellows at the top of her lungs. The wise canoeist runs for his life.

Just as every popular canoeing river in the country is mapped and charted, most of the rapids in them are also ranked according to the degree of difficulty they pose. The American White Water Association rates them as follows:

DIFFICULTY RATING

Class 1. Occasional small rapids with low regular waves not over one foot high. Course easily determined. Rescue spots all along. Shallow.

Class 2. More frequent rapids. Eddies and whirlpools offer no trouble. Ledges not over three feet high with a direct uncomplicated chute. Course easily determined. Waves up to three feet high but avoidable. Water more than three feet deep.

Class 3. Long rapids, maneuvering required. Course not easily recognizable. Waves up to five feet high, mostly regular, avoidable; strong cross currents; a good rescue spot after each rapid.

Class 4. Long rapids, intricate maneuvering. Course hard to determine, waves high (up to five feet) irregular, avoidable; or medium (up to three feet) and unavoidable; strong cross currents, eddies.

Class 5. Long continuous rapids, tortuous; requires frequent scouting. Extremely complex course. Waves large, irregular, unavoidable. Large scale eddies and cross currents. Rescue spots few and far off. Special equipment; decking, life jackets.

Class 6. Long continuous rapids without let-up. Very tortuous, always scout. Waves very high (above five feet), irregular, unavoidable; powerful cross currents. Special equipment; limit of canoeability, involves risk of life.

What makes the problem more difficult is that rivers and rapids change as water volume increases or declines. The average river in spring flood stage can offer many rapids in the Class 4 and 5 stage; in mountainous areas, add a few Class 6's to it. Yet when summer water levels do go down, the river is far gentler, the Class 4's and 5's being tamed into 1's and 2's.

How does one tell at what stage a river is? Observing it is no good unless the river is known in all its phases. However, it can be taken for granted that plenty of people are keeping close tabs on any river in the land. The Corps of Engineers has jurisdiction over many. Game wardens patrol others daily. Any fishing-tackle store owner knows the condition of local streams, and most can offer constructive advice on the dangers involved in running them at any given time.

SPECIAL WHITE-WATER EQUIPMENT

The cardinal rule every novice should burn into his mind is never to run dangerous stretches alone. Always proceed in company with other canoes and with a plan of rescue action decided upon before any trouble arises. For this reason, special safety equipment should be added to any canoe heading into white-water. Each boat should be equipped with 50 feet of ¼-inch rope. A high visibility blue or yellow polypropylene is best as it floats and can be readily spotted even in white foam. To one end attach an 18-inch throwing ring. This can be of light plastic, and in a pinch a preserver cushion is better than nothing. (Tie it through both straps.)

Another special item is a spare paddle. White-water lurches and shoves can easily snap canoe paddles, and unless another is available instantly the canoeist is helpless. The paddle should be lashed in with string sufficient to keep it in place in case of an upset, but light enough so a frantic pull can instantly tear it free.

Life preservers that can turn an unconscious person upright are another sensible precaution. The old "horse collar" is giv-

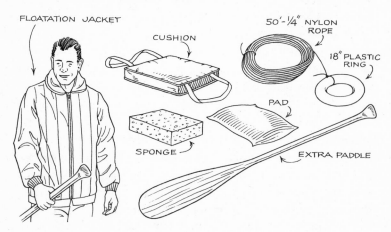

Special equipment desirable for safe white-water canoeing.

ing way to light garment-type flotation jackets that neither impair movements nor impart the pregnant-hippopotamus outline. Since in any dangerous rapids the proper technique is for both paddlers to be kneeling, knee pads can be used. If water is cold, heavy clothing should be worn. A skin diver's wet suit keeps the body warm even in freezing water.

A canoe for white-water should be without a keel or, at most, with only a "shoe" keel. It should have a pronounced bottom curve or "rocker." This enables the ends to turn quickly, and the lack of keel makes it possible for the boat to be moved bodily sideways by powerful draw or push strokes.

READING THE RAPIDS

Balancing its sinister danger is white-water's lack of mystery. A rapids is as easy to read as a first-grade primer. The rocks and ledges, boils and undercuts, cross-currents, and bends and twists that occur above and below the surface are all spelled out clearly on the river's surface. Fortunately, being able to identify the hazards all but disarms them.

It is a river characteristic that while rapids may contain boils and raging waves of such intensity no boat can live through them, adjacent to such places, often only feet away, can be found a path of water smooth enough for a Sunday School spinster to glide through. The trick is: first, finding the smooth path and, second, having the technical ability to position the canoe in it despite strong, often unexpected currents.

Any dangerous rapids should be scouted. The canoeist should walk the length of it, marking in his mind (and even in a sketchbook) where the hazards are and the exact route to follow to miss them. This may mean crossing at such and such a point, backwatering into a rest area, etc. He should figure where to dodge rocks and decide what "haystacks" can be met squarely and which must be skirted. Canoeists of great skill and experience can do this almost by instinct as they speed down an unfamiliar rapids. But note that the ACA ratings contain advice as to whether a given rapids should be scouted. It is a safe bet the experts study the bad ones carefully before plunging into them.

While coming down the rapids, the river ahead must be read from the small height the kneeling or sitting position allows. The skipper must know at all times at what point on his "chart" he is, not so easy in a long rapids. More important, the safe path ahead must be continually plotted and the canoe directed toward it. No words can substitute for on-stream reading lessons. However, there are some generalities.

Up & Down V's

V's with their point upcurrent, pointing toward the down-rushing canoe, are the enemy. V's where the wide angle of the V is upriver open their arms for the canoe to glide through and are friends.

A rock above water parts the water, making a white wave on either side that extends back past the rock in an ever-widening V like the wake of a ship. If the rock is below the surface, the V of the wake still shows. The deeper the rock, the farther back from it is the apex of the V.

Time and experience tell the canoeist where and how deep a rock is by the tiniest of signals. Does the water bulge slightly in front of the V? There is probably sufficient water to float the canoe over it. Is the bow wave a slow rumble that indicates deep water or an angry froth that means the rock looms close to the surface? Currents of varying intensities add to the difficulties of reading. A rock with 10 inches of water over it will give one signal in a current of 5 mph; another when the river flows at 10 mph; no signal at all if the current is nonexistent.

Conversely, while the captain of the canoe (he can be bowman or stern man, although usually the stern man is in command) avoids upstream V's, he seeks out downstream V's.

Most rapids are a series of obstacles that obstruct the flow of water in a chain of haphazard, inefficient dams. Water will start flowing for the dam opening well upstream of it, gradually constricting until it reaches the opening. The telltale V upstream sweeps the canoe into the deep safe slot.

"Haystacks" are large standing waves that form where water suddenly rushes from a shallow section into a much deeper area. These waves do not change position like ocean waves but froth and boil in the same spot constantly. There is usually good deep water under them. They pose problems only when they reach such size and intensity that the canoe cannot plow through them without taking on an undue amount of water. (If the bowman is a real expert, he will lean forward and slap his paddle from side to side to "flam" an open path through the frothy wave and prevent this.)

However, at times the waves become so big that they simply overpower any canoe not equipped with white-water decks. The boat hits a solid wall of water and scoops itself full even though it charges through the wave. Here, again, time and experience are the teachers. Although it is easiest to hit the haystack dead center (because the current there is swiftest), those that pose threats must be taken on the edge, the canoe scraping past the rocks along the side if necessary to avoid the water wall.

Currents

Most novices assume the current flows straight downstream, but nothing could be further from the truth. Any stretch of fast water contains side and back currents that the canoeist must recognize and use to his purpose. A back eddy makes a perfect spot to shoot *upstream* to safety. Yes, upstream.

In fact, safety much more often lies up a raging rapids than down. The reason is because every stretch of bad water automatically creates eddies behind it. These currents swing around toward shore, then upstream in a circle back to the main stream, and can readily be utilized to seek haven.

HOW TO ACQUIRE RIVER KNOW-HOW

The stream in spring is a most benevolent teacher, if the aspirant picks a gentle stream, and a most pleasant one. The hours spent observing the play of the bottom on the surface in ever bolder versions surely are the least wasted of all. Is there a rapids by a road nearby? The budding canoeist could do worse than observe it through four seasons; in his canoe in gentle season, from his car if weather and water turn unwelcome.

WHITE-WATER CANOE CONTROL

Once the white-water canoeist learns to see and identify the hazards so swiftly being served up to him, he must then have the skill to avoid them. The great risk is the canoe's grounding on a rock on one end or the other. If the stern section of the boat grounds, the results are not so instantly disastrous. The bow merely swings in line with the current, destroying whatever control was in effect or whatever maneuver was underway.

However, if the bow grounds, the effect is immediate. Instantly the stern swings sideways to the current, even 180°. In such an event, novice canoeists should swap positions. Both should turn in their seats, the bowman becoming stern man, but still in the bow. Such a maneuver will lift eyebrows among experts, but is far safer than attempting another 180° sweep to restore order.

Seldom is a river benign enough to permit such wild contortions without penalty. More often the canoe grounded at the bow never reaches the 180° turn. A rock or obstruction catches it somewhere along its length. The current then pins

If the bow of a canoe grounds in white water, the stern will start swinging sideways immediately. In the process, the hull may catch on some second obstruction.

the boat strongly against the obstructions. Ofttimes the boat capsizes somewhere in the process.

If it doesn't, what happens next depends on the particular situation. If the water is shallow enough, it's probably best for one man to get out and try to free the boat. If the water is deep, the boat can sometimes be pried off the rocks with paddles. In extreme cases, lines may have to be taken ashore, and with sunken canoes especially it is not uncommon for a boat to be pinned so strongly that such additional help will be needed to free it.

Iron control over the craft at all times is the method of avoiding such a gamut of horrors. At no time should the boat be allowed to take charge. It should be kept pointed straight up and down in the current, cocked never more than $30°$ from the straight line in the fast current during turns, draws, or sets.

The lone canoeist, of course, relies on his own assessment of the water and handles the boat as need be, usually from a kneeling position slightly aft of amidships. But two-man maneuvers require teamwork. Both paddlers must coordinate

In going through white water, keep tight control over the canoe's course at all times.

their efforts, often at split-second intervals. For this reason a set of commands should be agreed on before skills are put to the test. These need not be complicated: simple shouts of "back," "draw right," "set left" are sufficient if they clearly convey the skipper's intention and put two strong backs working to the same purpose.

HOLDING COURSE TO CLEAR AN OBSTACLE

Since the canoe seldom shoots straight down a stream, naturally it is sometimes difficult to determine exactly what course the boat is on and whether it will or will not clear an obstacle ahead. The way to tell quickly is to line the obstacle up with a mark on shore. If the mark and hazard stay aligned, the boat is on a collision course. If the two positions "open," the canoe will miss the hazard without effort on the part of the occupants.

HAZARDS AND EVASIVE TACTICS

Essentially, three basic tactics are utilized to avoid hazards. The first is obviously to steer the canoe around them. Oddly enough, this is not as easy as it sounds. In flat water a canoe steers well enough if the boat has fair speed through the water. A paddle used as a rudder turns it. But, immediately, this poses a problem in fast water.

While it is sometimes profitable for the canoe to careen down a rapids with the bowman paddling frantically to gain boat speed through the water so the stern man has steerage way, usually the reverse is desired. More often, the need is to slow the boat so the safe road ahead can be plotted and the boat positioned with care. Moreover, a canoe paddling down a current in a turn does not go in the direction it is pointed. At every moment the current is carrying it down while the effort is steering it sideways. The actual course then is a crabbed sweep, with the boat at an angle the whole time and, as such, always vulnerable to grasping underwater obstructions.

More useful are paddle strokes that will move or turn the boat when it is dead in the water. The draw or a combination of draw and push strokes are the most valuable. In these, both paddlers lean out, shove their paddles down as far right as they can, and pull toward the canoe with all their might. The effect is to jump the boat sideways a foot or two.

The push stroke, using the paddle as lever against the gunwale, is such an extremely powerful stroke that care must be taken not to snap the paddle. A series of draws and pushes by experts can make a canoe accelerate sideways with eye-opening speed.

How this works should be obvious. Either with both paddlers seeing obstacles or with one calling commands, the boat is moved sideways into safe paths. As an example, suppose an upstream V offers deep water, but immediately below the V slot is a rock. The boat shoots the slot. As it starts down, the stern man shouts, "Draw left."

Both men lean out and in, and three swift strong strokes simply move the canoe sideways far enough to shoot past the rock. Sounds easy, doesn't it? Yet play the scenario with variations. Suppose one man has no idea what the draw stroke is? How about if no one takes command and one man draws left, the other right? What if neither knows how to draw stroke, and the stern man tries to steer around the rock in the fast current? In all such cases, a canoe "horseshoed" around the rock can be forecasted.

"Setting" is a third evasive tactic. More than that, it is an escape route. It is the way the knowing canoeist lands or rests in fast water. Essentially, it employs frantic backing on the part of bow or stern man. But it is difficult to back a canoe in a straight line (try it in calm water sometime), so a long easy turn is the usual setting course. The maneuver is most effective when coordinated with a back eddy.

Let's say a particularly bad stretch has in its middle a huge rock. Water races around the rock, but behind it there is a quiet eddy. To race through the channel and attempt to turn the boat bow first into the eddy would be nearly impossible since much of the turning would have to be done in the fast water which would carry the boat far downstream. Look how setting solves the problem.

As the rock is approached, both paddlers frantically reverse, slowing the boat. The second the rock is past, the stern man backs and pushes or draws the boat's stern into the quiet water. The instant his paddle reaches that quiet water, the power of the current is vanquished. Since the distance between current rushing at 10 mph and dead quiet, or even turning slowly upstream is often measured in feet, sometimes inches, the set is extremely effective.

Most serious obstructions in a river offer quiet water havens behind them. Usually there is a circular current set up from water being drawn back upstream. In these the draw is used to yank the canoe out of the fast water. Caught in the upstream current, it is a simple matter to set the boat in toward the haven or shore stern first.

FENDING OFF

It is too much to expect that every rock can be missed. It is permissible (albeit poor form, like end swapping) to use the paddle to fend off rocks that should have been avoided by maneuvering. The bowman gets this assignment. There is no special art to it. He just sticks the blade against a point on the rock where he thinks it won't slip and throws his weight on the haft. The stern man should respond with a push or draw to move the whole boat in the direction away from the shove.

Grabbing branches is another common maneuver of dubious value. It greatly heightens the center of gravity because of the usual upward pull. A capsize here is hard to avoid. In any case, the stern man should always do the grabbing. If the bowman holds, the boat will certainly swing.

LINE AND PORTAGE

Lining a canoe means to draw or guide the craft less its passengers either up or downstream by the use of a line or lines— one usually attached low at the prow, the other at the stern.

Fending off during white-water passage. In fast water this calls for alertness at all times because there is usually only one right moment to fend off properly from each obstruction.

A canoe might have to be "lined" up or down a stretch of very shallow water, for instance. No hard and fast rule can be laid down about when to line and/or portage. (For techniques, see Chapter 7.) Everything depends so much on the individual situation. Some rivers are very difficult to line because of high banks. Others are easy. A portage consumes time; always extracts some cost in discomfort, insect attack, and so forth.

Certainly, the rule for novices should be never to enter any rapids above Class 2 which he has not scouted in advance. If on the scouting party he feels any hesitation, opt for the safer route. Similarly if there is much at stake, much equipment, small children, unusual hazards, the safer path should be adopted.

SPILLS AND OTHER DANGERS

One of the most important white-water rules the beginning canoeist should always remember is to resist the normal urge —when the boat is sweeping down sideways against a rock— to lean the boat on the upstream side. It invariably appears that hitting the rock will tip the boat by stopping the bottom and that the inertia of the boat's movement will then capsize it. This ignores the current, of course, which is the determining factor.

But tipping the upstream side merely increases the boat's underwater area and thus increases the current's push against it, pinning the boat strongly and often capsizing it. However, if the canoe is tipped *toward* the approaching rock, the effect will be to send the current under the boat as it pushes the upstream side even higher, decreasing its force. Thus the current lifts the boat, often freeing it without further effort by the occupants.

Waterfalls are such obvious danger points that it is a wonder that every year canoes continue to get swept over them. The "boil" beneath the falls and in certain other deep spots in rivers, may trap swimmers by drawing them down time and again by the circular current.

Here, as when being swept against a rock, the swimmer should go against his instincts and dive instead of struggling for the top. The strongest currents sweep the bottom and will shoot him into the clear. Simple scouting or reading a map of the river reveals waterfalls well in advance, of course. The boat should be landed well upcurrent and the falls portaged.

Trees fallen across a stream pose a greater problem than most canoeists realize, for several reasons. Unlike rapids or falls, they do not advertise their presence by sound. Nor do they obstruct stream flow. If they topple into a fast stretch, the stretch stays just as fast. This obstruction neither slows the current, nor often offers any place to dodge. Finally, trees may fall at any time and are seldom mapped. The canoeist rounds a bend and is surprised.

Defense depends on the situation. Perhaps the boat can sneak under a spot or over a submerged portion. Often a quick set to land is required, followed by some axe work.

CAPSIZES AND SWAMPING

The vital rule to remember is that if the canoe does capsize, never get downstream in front of it. Duck under it or hold position so it goes past.

Also, swimmers are safer to stay with a swamped canoe than to abandon it. The accepted procedure is to grab the stern and ride the boat down through the rapids as if swimming a horse, holding the stern to keep the boat straight.

Oddly, because of its now greater depth, the boat directed this way will in uncanny fashion seek the deeper water and often glide through bad stretches with amazing ease. If the canoe cannot be reached, swimmers should face downstream on their backs, feet first, treading water until a calm is reached.

Often canoes become trapped against rocks and must be

manhandled off. Small saplings can be cut to serve as levers. Ropes may be tied together and to a tree, and a Spanish windlass set up. Usually, several individuals heaving at one end will jockey the boat around enough so that the current's grip is broken.

ADVANCE WHITE-WATER TECHNIQUES

If the challenge of white-water grows, there is much beyond that beckons. The addition of a spray deck adds much seaworthiness to the white-water canoe.

For experts only are the so-called "banana" boats and single-man canoes and kayaks. These are fully decked with the occupant sitting in a single cockpit (double in the C1 and C2 canoes) with full watertight integrity achieved by a skirt held on the cockpit lip with elastic cord. Tremendous rough water ability is then achieved. A whole host of new techniques—lean-turns, Eskimo-rolls—opens in this exciting new world which, at the moment, the beginner must look at and admire from afar.

About as watertight as he can make it, this kayaker has his cockpit skirt fastened snugly in preparation for rough water. Rigged this way, many kayakers find much sport in boating often rough ocean shoreline waters.

CHAPTER SEVEN

Transporting and Portaging

There's an exhilaration, a rhythm, and a fierce clean freedom to canoeing, especially in the unfrequented places, that lifts it out of the realm of all other sports and separates its enthusiasts into a dedicated clan.

Nothing brings one more alert. Every muscle responds instantly, with both power and delicacy, to the swiftly shifting demands of balance and steerage. One poises, almost quivering with restrained energy, studying which bulge of water to ride around an onrushing boulder. Then he's driving the blade with fast, hefty jabs. He's fighting to swing the stern free of a suddenly chortling current that hungers to heave the craft broadside up against the froth-whitened projection and there snap it in two.

Then with a sudden plunge and lift he's past. Immediately he is fairly met with another challenge to every last shred of

strength, judgment, and skill—and another and another. He
eyes ahead, braces himself, and turns his instantaneous deci-
sions into exultant action amid the hiss of wind and contest-
ing water.

Then the canoe is through the last of this racing turmoil.
The stream widens into a deep gentleness. It is so abruptly
quiet that when the paddle scrapes a gunwale the brief clatter
seems a desecration, although one realizes the current is merely
bunching behind another rock-pierced channel somewhere
ahead. He sees the perfect birch under which to spread his
bedroll. His legs shake a little when he steps ashore. He draws
in a deep breath. He's ten feet tall.

But two problems remain: getting the canoe and outfit to
the point of embarkation and carrying it around unnavigable
stretches.

CARTOPPING THE CANOE

With two people there isn't any problem in putting a canoe on
car racks. They just lift and slide it on.

One man may have a problem, though. A stern outboard
bracket is an assist. This, because of its flat surface, allows one
end of the canoe to be picked up without the craft's pivoting
on its sharp point at bow or stern.

Very important in cartopping singlehanded is a roll bar.
This is a bar that connects the front and rear rack. One lifts
one end up on the bar, then hoists the other end, slides the
canoe about halfway at a 90° angle to the way the boat will
finally ride, and then swings the end around so the canoe lies
fore and aft on horizontal racks. Reverse to unload.

If the after-crossbar is located far enough toward the rear
of the car, one can put one end of the canoe on it, then go
around, pick up the other end, and slide the boat forward into
position. The thing about the roll bar—or the end rack which

The average canoe can easily be put up on cartop bars by two people.

does not work on most cars, even the roofs of the modern station wagons slanting too much to make it practical—is that one only has to pick up one-half the canoe at a time. And one always maintains control, which can be important if the wind is blowing. Say the canoe weighs 130 pounds. Then with the roll bar the packer lifts only 65 pounds or less at a time because one end of the boat is always supported on either the ground or the roll bar.

Two-canoe rigs are easy on a car. One can even sandwich a third canoe on top of the pair, using life-preserver cushions to cradle the boat. Beforehand, though, both racks must be lengthened.

Plenty of canoes, too, are carried on cars without racks. Most of these travelers just rest them on cushions and lash down. This is risky, though, as the wind is always lifting and lightening that boat, and the cushions can then easily blow away, whereupon the roof of the car catches it. Still, many travel this way.

Canoes should be lashed to the racks and additionally secured by ropes fore and aft to the bumpers. The front line is
the more important, as the wind gets under the bow and tends
to lift it. Canoe beams are around 40 inches, incidentally, and
standard racks a comfortable 60 inches, so the load is an easy
one.

Racks

By far the best cartop rack is made by Quik-N-Easy in
Monrovia, California. This bolts to car gutters, then clamp-on
bars bolt to it. L. L. Bean of Freeport, Maine 04032 sells it
by mail, postpaid, for $25.50 for a 60-inch crossbar and
$28.50 for a 78-inch crossbar. A roll bar costs $8.50.

The second best kind of racks are those that fit down into
the car gutters and clamp there.

Suction-cap racks are cheap and common, but hitting
bumps can depress them. This puts slack in the ties that hold
the clamps in the gutter. The wind can then blow the clamp
out, whereupon off comes the rack. The solution? Big shock
cords between the hold-down straps to keep constant tension
on them.

Lashing The Canoe Down

In addition to having well secured bow and stern lines, any
canoe loaded for cartopping must be solidly secured to the
carrying bars (or cartop), a requirement usually adequately
met by fastening two strong web straps across the canoe bottom, their ends anchored to the carrying bars. There is much
room for improvisation here, it being relatively easy to rig
quick-detachable/attachable fastenings which make canoe tie-
down and dismounting a swift and simple job, particularly
appreciated by those who cartop their craft frequently. In lieu
of using heavy-duty straps—and few of the carrying bar kits

contain straps of desirable strength and width—the canoe can be merely lashed down securely. Some canoeists employ a crisscross X lashing. A good way of getting lines like this secure is to tie a bowline in one end, then to use that loop like a pulley to pull the line tight. Then with the rope pinched around the loop to maintain tension, throw a half hitch in the free end. One can pinch the loop and bring the hitch up snug before any slackening occurs.

Whether a canoe has been well tied down or not will quickly become apparent upon traversing a stretch of washboard road.

VIA RAILROAD OR AIR

Most Canadian railways will carry a canoe, stopping anywhere to pick up or let off. This is an uncommon practice in the U.S. Across the North the bush pilots will fly canoes and outfits in and out anywhere.

PORTAGING

When it comes to portaging, discretion continues to be the better part of valor, especially when one is more or less a greenhorn in this new canoeing world. Particularly when a trail around rapids seems to be well traveled, it will be well to heed such eloquent counsel.

On most canoe trips of any length, one or more portages will be necessary, perhaps a carry from one lake to another or an overland route around a stretch of white water. If it is not exceptionally windy and one is traveling, as he should be, light, then the work will not be too strenuous, even when one is alone. In fact, it often feels good to get out and stretch one's legs.

Ideally, it will be possible to complete a portage in two carries. On the first trip over, carry the packs. At that time, armed with an axe, it will be possible to scout out the trail and to clear away any obstructions. Finally, come through with the canoe itself.

Perhaps the carry will come at tea time. Then build the lone bright fire at the other end. It is both a psychological and physiological mistake to rest *before* a portage. For one thing, muscles stiffen. For another, the task looms all the more formidable. To boil the kettle is all the more gratifying when all that remains to be done, first making sure that every last spark is extinguished, is to board the portaged and repacked canoe and set forth once more.

If one is traveling with a map, portages will be marked. Otherwise, stop and look for them at the sound of white water. The portage trail, if any, will be along the line of easiest going. It may, of course, be on either side of the stream, especially if that is on the inside of a bend. A landing place is usually obvious, perhaps because of tracks, or clearing, or dead fires, or even litter.

In crossing overland from one lake to another, look for a dip in the hills. The earliest individuals to use such a portage wanted to make it as easy as possible. In the old days, such portages were frequently marked by blazes or by lopping off the higher branches of a conspicuously high tree, some of which still stand.

Shoulder Protection

The most arduous portage begins with one step, and even that will be more comfortable to take when some provision is made for padding between the canoe and the shoulders. This may be only the flats of the lashed paddles, plus a folded extra shirt.

Stores and outfitters also sell aluminum, plastic, and hardwood yokes to ease portaging problems. These go on the inside of the canoe in the center, so that on balance the bow will lift a bit higher than the stern. But they are one more item to carry.

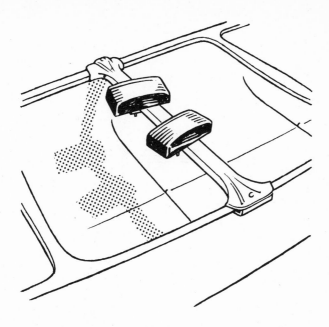

Commercial-type yoke for canoe portage use.

With most canoes one can make his own yoke by lashing two paddles between the thwarts, preferably so that the flat portion of the blade will rest against the shoulders on balance, the stern again slightly lower than the prow, making it handier to lift the forward end for better vision. When there is a center thwart, this is no problem. If the paddles must be secured instead to bow and stern thwarts, it may be the slim parts of the paddles that will meet the shoulders, in which case one will want plenty of padding.

In any event, the yoke should be well secured. Any slipping would not only be uncomfortable, but it could be downright hazardous. Caution should be exercised on all carries so as to avoid falls and sprains. Incidentally, bugs may be a bother when one is occupied in keeping the canoe balanced on his shoulders. During fly seasons, apply plenty of repellent, for

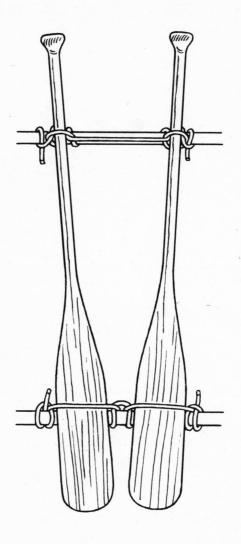

Portage yoke fashioned by tying canoe paddles to thwarts.

few things are more distracting than mosquitoes whining in the enclosed stuffiness directly over the imprisoned head.

On short carries with light canoes that have a central thwart, the voyageur frequently does not bother with any yoke, merely upturning the craft over his head and resting the thwart against his neck.

As for tiny canoes, these can be transported under an arm.

On short carries, too, the lightweights are sometimes carried upright and unpacked by two men, the keel resting on the shoulders. It then becomes all the more important for the partners to maintain the same rhythm in walking, usually a process that requires considerable concentration because of the unevenness of the ground. A good waltzer has more luck in carrying a canoe, as a gliding walk rather than a bouncy stride helps keep the weight from continually jabbing into the neck and shoulders.

Lifting

The secret lies in tossing instead of pressing. With one man, roll the emptied and upright canoe away from one's self on one side and take hold of the yoke or the center thwart. With an upward jerk of the arm and a forward shove of the knees, toss the craft up and around. The knees support the bulge of the canoe briefly when it is halfway up. Then when the craft is tossed and bounced nearly upside down, duck the head beneath into its position in front of the yoke or center thwart. This way, the two hands and the knees will get the canoe up without straining or even overexerting the back and arms.

When two partners are involved, the lift is easy. Again, the canoe is started right-side-up. The bowman stands slightly ahead of the front seat, the stern man a bit ahead of the rear seat. Each bends down and grips the gunwales. Then, on signal, they lift together, rolling the canoe over as it is hoisted. The seats themselves can then become the carrying yokes.

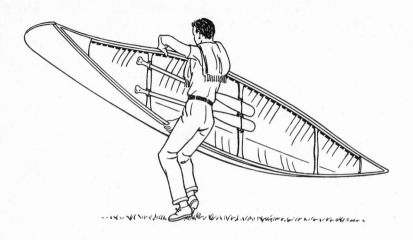

Lifting canoe in preparation for portage—one man.

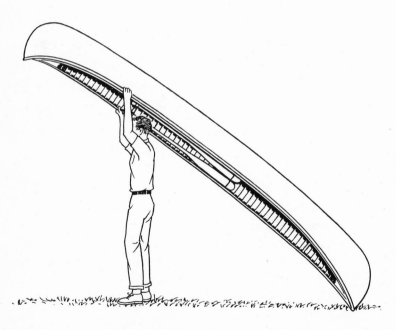

Lifting canoe when readying to load on car top or to put in portage carry position.

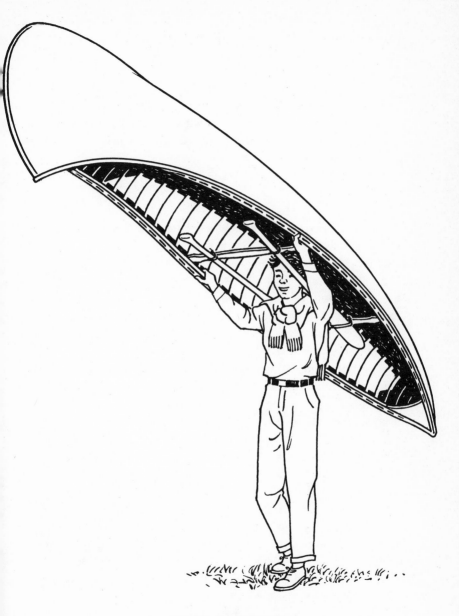

Portaging—one-man carry.

The greenhorn working by himself can, until he gains experience, instead prop the bow against a rock or tree, get in position under the thus half-raised canoe, and easily bring it in balance across his shoulders and neck. When one man will be carrying the canoe, the other the duffle, then the second canoeist himself can half-lift the craft for his partner.

With a carry longer than 50 yards, some sort of padding will make things a lot easier. Many a canoeist just puts on his down jacket.

Tump Line

Tump lines used to be widely used for portaging. These are long lines with a center band of leather or canvas that, once the tump line is tied into position, can rest on the forehead or head. There must be enough slack so that the head neither hits the canoe bottom nor is held too uncomfortably high. With experience, a tump line can be an asset, and one is frequently used to capitalize on the neck's and upper shoulders' strength in company with a regular or improvised yoke.

The tump line today consists of a broad band of thick, soft leather about 3 inches wide and 15 inches long. Canvas is sometimes used instead. To each end of this headpiece is attached something such as a rope or rawhide thong perhaps 10 feet long. Tapering straps are so employed, too, their length being adjustable by buckles.

When duffle is being transported, the two extremities are secured to the bundle to be packed in such a way that at the proper height above the bundle the headband forms a loop. This usually goes over the forehead at about the natural hairline, while the bundle rests against the middle of the back just over the hips. The weight is thus supported by the head, the neck muscles, and the spinal column. It is steadied by pressure on the shoulders, back, and hips.

The sportsman will find the tump line a vexing way of pack-

The tump line and how it is used.

ing until he develops strength and endurance in his neck muscles. He should never attempt it, except experimentally, on his first outdoor journey. But if he is to continue taking canoe vacations year after year, he may well learn to use this flexible accessory, for with it a greater weight can be packed than in any other manner.

The base to which the tump line is attached often consists of a roll of bedding or a sack of flour. This rests low down, almost on top of the hips. When it is in place, other bundles such as flour sacks, duffle bags, and loose articles of most any kind are piled on top. Reaching in some instances almost to the top of the packer's head, these go more or less between the two lines stretching from the base bundle to the headpiece. The packer keeps everything in place by bending slightly forward. It's not as difficult to balance the load as one might expect.

In this manner, professional Indian and half-breed packers regularly used to take freight weighing up to 200 pounds over portages up in the Hudson's Bay Company country. One weight record was held by a big Cree Indian named Joe Morin who, in a contest between some Chippewayan and Cree packers at Pelican Narrows in Manitoba, carried for 100 yards the incredible weight of 620 pounds of flour.

The tump line is at its best for short distances on plainly marked portages. Its advantages are too often offset when one has to pick his way over rough ground, for the head is bent downward in such a way that one can not turn it without swinging his entire body. Therefore, he can not easily see what lies ahead, nor can he spot game. Even if he did glimpse a retreating bruin, he could not get off a well-aimed shot while movement and vision were so restricted.

The tump line's chief value lies in the fact that with it more can be taken over the portage in one trip. Only one tump line per man is needed. It is simply untied from one load and hitched to the next.

PACKSACKS FOR PORTAGING

The other form of pack in most common use among experienced canoeists is the packsack variously known by such names as the Duluth, Poirier, Woods, Maine, and Northwestern. Basically, it is merely a canvas sack or bag, approximately 15 to 20 inches wide and 25 to 30 inches long, opening at the top. Shoulder straps extend from a central point at the top to the two bottom corners.

Many outfitters make it up in a reinforced boxlike bag of waterproofed duck, about 18 by 26 by 8 inches. Extra pockets are sometimes sewed on the outside and in the flap that covers the square top opening. In addition, provision is frequently made for attaching a tump line to buckles or D rings on the outer edges of the sack near the top. Use of the tump line is optional.

Camp duffle and grub are stowed inside the sack up to its capacity in weight or bulk, soft materials nearest the back and lighter goods at the bottom. One packsack commonly carries all cooking and eating utensils, as well as victuals to be used for the next meal. On arrival at the new camp, this is deposited near the site for the fire so the cook can get busy pronto.

Blankets can be folded and packed inside a sack, and so can the tent or shelter cloth. But, commonly, these are rolled and the bundle balanced on top of a fully loaded packsack where it is easily carried. Rations and other essentials are frequently packed in waterproof duffle bags, about 9 by 24 inches, which are supplied by most camp outfitters. These bags can also be conveniently balanced atop the pack.

As the shoulder straps may at times have to bear a considerable weight, they should be broad where they go over the shoulders. It is also a good thing to pad them with something such as sheepskin to which the fleece remains attached. The tump line may be used to take some of the heft off the shoulder straps. In fact, employing the support in this manner is the easiest way to get the hang of using it alone.

A mighty good pack for those kitchen goods is the old-fashioned pack basket, once so popular in northern New York and Maine. Strong and resilient, it protects breakable and crushable objects from being jammed together, at the same time riding easily on the back. In camp, it can be hung in a shady place along with perishables that need coolness and ventilation. The bedroll perches so easily on top of such a basket that the two combine to make a load that's light enough for almost anyone.

Many other types of packs can be used for carrying fairly heavy loads short distances. Steer clear of those which have the shoulder straps attached far apart at the top of the sack. These will be continually slipping down on the arms. Shoulder straps should start very close together from the top of the pack, even from a single large D ring. Those of thick, oil-tanned leather are far superior to webbing.

The Bergans type of frame rucksack and the Alaskan pack board, so ideal for backpacking vacations, are excellent for canoeing. Even though the former can not very well have bags piled atop it, one is convenient for packing valuables such as camera and binoculars that have been safely tied within partially inflated plastic bags, and indispensables such as fishline, hooks, and perhaps a small supply of ammunition. One can stow this under his seat, snapping or buckling one strap fast if he wants. If it will float, and a sealer cloth at the open end may be enough to secure this, the better procedure may be to leave it free. Either way, one can get at it in a hurry if need be.

Probably the only reason why the especially adaptable pack board has not become widely popular among canoeists is because it has not yet really reached the northeastern canoe country. It certainly is the best way to pack hard and unwieldy objects, particularly outboard motors. Instead, these last are often wrapped in some impervious cover and then in a tent, and packed with the tump line. Too, one sometimes sees ingenious packs designed to carry a particular kicker.

Cans of gas and oil are often tied to each end of an eight-foot pole, and the pole then balanced over one shoulder in the

Chinese coolie fashion. Loose articles such as guns, rods, and axes are carried by hand. It is not uncommon to note a bucket, filled with most anything, also so borne.

HAVE A SYSTEM

Anything one wants to get during the day, such as lunch or boiling kettle, tuck conveniently into a side space. Cameras and fishing gear should also be accessible. Tents and water-proofs should be on the outside of rolls and packs in case camp has to be made in a downpour. If one figures he is going to need his down jacket, wedge it under the bow or stern deck where it can be gotten at easily.

The first individual across a portage should bring an axe in case any cutting has to be done. The fellow whose job it is to tote the canoe should go over a strange carry first with a pack to become familiar with it. When he takes the canoe over, another packer should go along with him if possible.

If two travelers with a lightweight canoe can reduce their duffle to just three packs, each of which they can carry without undue effort, the work of portaging will be greatly simplified. They'll then have to make but two trips. Each will take a pack load on the first. On the second, one will bring a pack and help the other where he can with the canoe.

Whether one adopts these methods of packing and handling the outfit, or has the fun of devising a routine of his own, adhere to a system. Have a place for everything and everything in its place. It means less labor, delay, and confusion in travel-ing and in camp, and one has more time to devote to the plain pleasures of living.

Such a system also eases most of the drudgery out of portag-ing. It can even make a carry something to look forward to as a break in the monotony of paddling, an opportunity to stretch the legs, and in chilly weather a chance for some welcome exercise; all provided there are no confounded bugs. Skeeters and black flies, unless one has one of the better modern repellents, can turn a portage into something else again. But the modern voyageur will soon forget any discomfort at the next glittering challenge of open water.

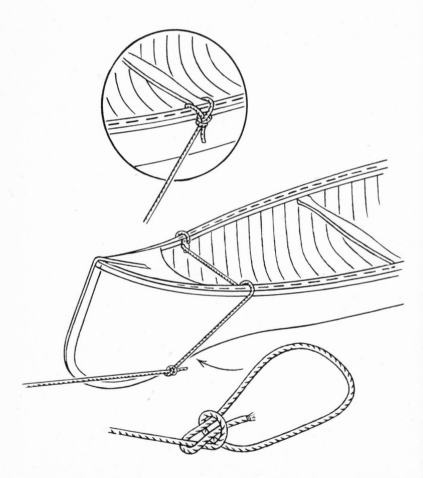

Attaching lines in preparation for lining a canoe. In this case the lines are rigged for lining a canoe downstream. If a canoe is to be lined upstream, the lines would be rigged to keep the bow up (rigged the reverse of that shown here).

LINING THE CANOE

The major secret in lining is to get the front rope hauling the canoe just above the waterline. This can be accomplished most conveniently from a ring attached to this outward portion of the bow. Lacking this, run a rope around the boat, top and bottom, and tie the line to the under center of this. Both of these methods will cause the bow to lift slightly under pressure, as it should; this also being the correct method of tying on for

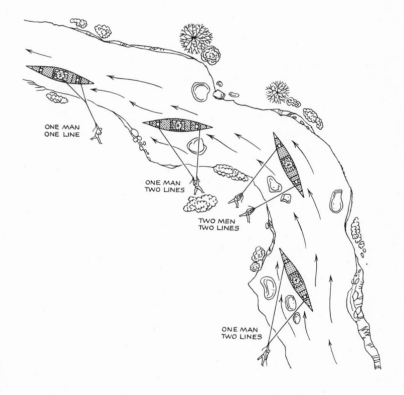

Illustrating methods of lining a canoe. If the stream banks are unobstructed, two canoeists could perhaps work farther apart than suggested here.

towing. When, as is usually done instead, the line is attached to the gunwale, the bow dips and ploughs erratically.

When two men are lining a canoe, they'll also need a stern line, a good provision even with one man. Depending on the water, both of these can be up to about 100 feet long. Then, walking or wading as best one can along the shore, the one or two individuals pull the floating, usually loaded craft through an otherwise unnavigable stretch of water. When the duffle is left in the canoe, incidentally, it should be centered low in the craft so that the canoe can spin easily at either end.

Using the current and the ropes, the canoeist—or two of them—can steer the craft to a certain extent. Pulling on the bow and easing the tension on the stern will cause the craft to move shoreward. The opposite of this, a tight stern and a loose bow, will urge the canoe outward.

Despite all this, the maneuver becomes tricky at times, and either or both individuals may also carry a pole with which to fend off the canoe. Too, the second partner sometimes rides the canoe with a pole, although balance then usually becomes a considerable problem.

Canoes are also lined downstream, whereupon most of the brawn is used in holding them back.

CHAPTER EIGHT

Favorite Floats

Not far from the reader are canoeing waters of inestimable worth. They are pure and clean, filled with everything from trout to bass of both varieties and fighting pike, and during these harried days, especially luring. While on some a few cottages and campsites dot the banks, most are still amazingly remote, affording the unique thrill of leaving civilization behind.

In addition to offering the priceless opportunity of getting back to nature, each waterway described in the following has one vastly important element in common. All are public property. They are wide open. Indeed, most are being preserved inviolate, locked away from the rapacious hand of man. Not only have their sparkling waters been acclaimed the continent's best, but they're remaining that way. These are truly favorite floats, known, used, and enjoyed by thousands back into the dim history of the past; managed and preserved so that they are waiting to offer their charm to thousands to come. Like the reader!

These favorite floats have been picked with several things in mind. First, of course, each had to be famous for scenic beauty and great fishing. Second was availability. Each had to be public property—or treated as such.

And they had to be safe. No great canoe expertise should be required to float them beyond the willingness of procuring readily available maps, using these, and exercising reasonable common sense and prudence.

On a couple of waters the simplest compass skill is needed, as "find the northwest side of a lake." Proof of their gentle nature had to be that all would have to be floated many times by first timers to canoe camping. All easily qualify.

The next requirement was that on none would it be necessary to invest one penny in equipment of one's own. Outfitters in quantity had to be offering for rental everything but personal clothing: canoe, tent, sleeping bag, pots and pans, and even basic food for the time the individual planned to be gone—everything. There were two reasons for this: first, that this book is designed to attract people to trying a float of their own; second, even if one has his own equipment, he can benefit from these outfitters' capacity to solve put-in and take-out transportation problems. Too, they are the best source of detailed information on the waters they know so well.

Costs of rental gear are modest, by the way. Figure about $10 a day per person if all gear, including food, is supplied. Canoe rental is about $7 a day tops, a good-sized tent $3 daily, sleeping bag $2, and so forth.

Another requirement was geographical distribution. The waters had to be so scattered that no matter where the reader lives one would be reasonably close. Only the West Coast is excluded, and the omission is not serious in view of the surfeit there of floatable steelhead rivers.

The last test each waterway had to pass was that inexpensive literature, describing each in detail, had to be readily available.

Instead of being just armchair-stuff that dreams are made of, although potent medicine in that department, this literature is detailed enough so that with it, and some local advice on camp sites, one can actually travel the route.

For those who desire a more detailed overview of America's numerous canoeing water ways, the book *Introduction to Water Trails in America* by Robert Colwell (Stackpole Books) is suggested. In this volume the author takes the reader along on most of the floats covered and actually describes the scenery as it unfolds along the way, even suggesting various places to camp enroute. Its value in trip planning is hence out of the ordinary.

A final note . . . Remember that a canoe trip on any of these waters is not just another outdoor jaunt. A wilderness float is like a safari or ocean cruise. It's an experience that sticks to the ribs. Not being altogether predictable, it therefore becomes unforgettable. It never fades from memory. Those days and nights will live with one forever.

MICHIGAN'S AU SABLE

Long one of the most famous trout streams in the country, this super-popular river has lost much of its pristine wilderness character, but thanks to donations—one man who loved the river presenting a 14-mile stretch of its bank to the public— and the commendable recreational policy of the Consumer's Power Company who make over 100 miles of river frontage available to canoe campers and fishermen, the Au Sable very much earns a place among the world's best.

The river bank teems with wildlife, scars of the lumbering industry have healed, and the broad free-flowing stream with few dam portages and no white water is perfect for family canoeing with a trout fisherman in charge. One will find summer evenings on the river when trout dapple the surface everywhere. In the backwaters of the dams, bass and Northerns can be had. Numerous campgrounds make selection of the night's campsite easy. Access points are plentiful, and at most canoes and all gear can be easily obtained.

Reece Fabbro, owner of Ohio Canoe Adventurers Inc., Box 2092, Sheffield Lake, Ohio 44054 is an Au Sable expert. His favorite stretches are from Grayling to Mio, and from Roscommon on the South Branch through the Mason Grant wilderness to the main stream and then down to Mio. The best way to start a trip down the legendary Au Sable is to send $2 to Mr. Fabbro for his excellent description of the entire stream with camping, fishing, and access details.

Stream liveries include Bay's Canoe Livery, Carr's Pioneer Canoes, Carlisle Canoes, all of Grayling, Michigan 49738; Mio Sport Shop, Mio, Michigan 48647, and Lovell's Canoe Rental, Oscoda, Michigan 48750. Johnboats and cartoppers can also float the Au Sable.

ONTARIO'S ALGONQUIN PROVINCIAL PARK

Set aside in 1893, this 3000-square-mile wilderness area 100 miles northeast of Toronto is probably the second-most popular canoeing region in the world. Only Quetico-Superior, which it resembles, can beat it.

This is the real Canadian bush. The wolves howl at night, deer drink at lakeside, beaver lodges abound. It is typical terrain of the Ontario watery ways. One lake piles on another, often tied together with streams, always linked by portages that range from a few feet long to over a mile. Park rangers have set out 15 canoe routes that vary in distance from 35 to 175 miles; most around 40 to 50 miles, an easy week's trip with plenty of time for attacking the lake and brook trout, bass, and muskies plentiful in all the lakes.

For the last few years some 35,000 canoeists annually have let Algonquin Park's balmy breezes soothe city-wearied spirits.

There are two outfitters offering gear and access to the interior from paved highway 60. Canadian Railways bisects the park and will drop off or stop for a canoe party anywhere along its right-of-way.

The way to start into Algonquin is by writing for the excellent free map of the park with detailed information about everything one can think of on the back. Address T. W. Hueston, Superintendent, Algonquin Provincial Park, Algonquin Park Post Office, Ontario, Canada. Fees are modest, a 16-day camp permit costing $5.

There are two outfitters who offer canoes at $24 a week as well as any other gear one might need. To start planning a jaunt during July or August and setting a canoe reservation, drop everything and immediately ship off $4, a day's rental fee, to the Portage Store Supplies, Mr. K. Simpson, 68 Forest Grove Drive, Willowdale, Ontario until May, thereafter to Portage Store Supplies, Canoe Lake P.O., Ontario. Or, Bill Swift, Algonquin Outfitters, RR1, Dwight, Ont. Some 400 canoes are available for rental, but reservations for the summer months are needed. Don't forget, too, the reasonableness of renting a canoe locally and cartopping it to wherever one wants to go.

QUETICO-SUPERIOR WATERWAYS

Somehow it's always impressive that canoe nuts have a gigantic wilderness area reserved for them alone. And so zealously guarded that airplanes can't fly over it lower than 4,000 feet!

Does a secret canoe lobby stalk Congressional halls like the highway lobby, banking lobby, et al? If so, they function in Canada, as the Quetico portion of the 14,500-square-mile, roadless, houseless virgin land of lakes, trees, streams, and God's wild creatures exists in that country. Quetico is an Ontario Provincial Park, Superior a U.S. National Forest.

Some of God's wild creatures one can expect to view are other canoeists—in plenty. Some 113,000 checked in the year before this book was written, and while there are 1200 miles of canoe routes in Superior alone, everybody wants to travel the same ones.

Last summer Forest personnel started regulating for the first time who could go where, when. In fact they prefer *not* to publicize the park to avoid crowding, a typical approach to the problem which one would believe might easily be solved by opening other areas such as they have done in the Crane Lake area. Enabling legislation has passed to create Voyageur National Park. Its boundaries abut the present park, and one can go there and run back and forth over the near-vertical Grand Portage to get in shape. The voyageurs often made the 36-mile round trip in 6 hours, carrying two 90 pound packs!

As the canoeist would expect, this is true wilderness with all it offers. Northern pike and walleyes everywhere await lures. If one has any sense of history, it will thrill him to see rocks worn smooth by the moccasined feet of the voyageurs and, for eons before them, Indians. Yet with the sense of distance, because both areas are officially administered, in any emergency a U.S. or Canadian ranger is never far away.

There are three good access points into Superior; in Ely, Grand Marais, and Crane Lake. Ely is by far the most popular. In fact, many don't even know the others exist. Canadian access is desirable if one wants solitude, as not many make the 100-mile drive to enter from the north at French Lake on Route 11 east of Atikan. One can also enter Quetico through several other lakes on Route 11 and via Crane Lake where a right turn will put one quickly in Canada.

There is excellent free literature from Supervisor, Superior National Forest, Box 338, Duluth, Minnesota 55801 or District Forester, Dept. Lands and Forests, Ft. Francis, Ontario, Canada.

Two minor points are not generally known. Snowmobile trails have been laid out in both areas, and both contain miles of canoe trails on which outboard motors are allowed.

THE UPPER DELAWARE

The Delaware River, despite its proximity to a third of the nation's population, remains amazingly pristine and unspoiled along its upper length. Admittedly there are cabins along its bank, a scruffy town or two, and there are beer cans, people, and highways along the shore that intrude. Yet, despite them, the water is pure and sweet. Smallmouth and lunker walleyes make the river famous in successive springs and falls. When the spring run is on, all hands in the area turn out to try for the shad that somehow manage to make it through the inhuman pollution of the river below Trenton.

The general impression of a Delaware float is wilderness. One's eyes climb to the forested ridges where limestone cliffs sheltered the Indians that roamed the river as early as 10,000 years ago. What has saved the river is limited access. There still aren't very many spots where one can launch a boat.

Most of the Pennsylvania side is heavily timbered with no access points. And spots to launch on New York and New Jersey shores are few and far between, made to order for canoe floats. For them the river is perfect, with plenty of current, few portages, and only three or four dangerous rapids on a 60-mile floatable stretch.

While there are few public campsites, wilderness banks make camping easy on private lands. This section of the Delaware contains authentic geological wonders, including the famed Water Gap where the river has carved its way through a gigantic wall of rock that, if one thinks it looks impressive from the road, he should view from a canoe. As one gets closer to Trenton, the current slows and the wilderness aspect gives way to sleepy little villages with much charm.

Probably the most popular float is from Narrowsburg to Barryville. From Callicoon to Narrowsburg the river offers true wilderness but doesn't get as much attention, as a portage at a falls is necessary.

An excellent map of the Delaware, suitable for running it, can be obtained for $1 from the Delaware River Basin Commission, 25 Scotch Road, Suburban Square, Trenton, N.J. Canoe outfitters include: Bob Landers, Minisink Ford Canoe, Barryville, N.Y. 12719; Hillside Inn, Route 97, Narrowsburg, N.Y.; Kittstinny Canoes, Silver Lake Road, Dingmans Ferry, Pa. 18328; Bob's Beach, Milford, Pa. 18337. It's great water, too, for cartoppers and johnboats.

MISSOURI'S CURRENT RIVER

"No U.S. canoeist has arrived until he has taken the Current River trip," writes our friend Charlie Moore, founder of the United States Canoe Association.

Here is an Ozark float at its best; camps along gravel bars, high cliffs, gentle climate with one group even featuring an annual New Year's Day float, and sizzling rock and small-mouth bass fishing. The Current is free of rapids. Some riffles and turns present the only danger, along with the possibility of being swept under an overhanging tree, a traditional Ozark float hazard.

The most heavily traveled section of the river is from Akers Ferry to around Big Spring State Park, a 75-odd-mile trip that makes a great week's float. A 10 miles-a-day speed allows plenty of time to work the fishy spots. Float fishing tip? Make one's distance in the middle of the day. Fish hard in the morning until about 10 a.m., work hard across the noon hours, and then make camp in the afternoon in a spot where there will be fishing after supper.

The Current has Quetico-Superior's problem. Too many people! Since its designation as a National Wild Riverway, the number of people floating has increased spectacularly. "It's floated so much the water shows worn spots," one Ozarkian says. Some form of quota system seems to be in the offing and the canoeist should take this into his planning. The warm springs and open falls of the South suggest that one should try to schedule his float on this, one of the world's most beautiful rivers, during off-season.

The Missouri Department of Conservation, 2901 Ten Mile Drive, Jefferson City, Mo. 65101, offers fair, free maps and information on the Current. Ohio Canoe Routes has a better guide to all Missouri waterways for $1.50. A sampling of many outfitters includes Jadwin Canoe Rental, Highway 19, Salem, Mo. 65560; Current River Resort, Gladden, Mo. 65478; and Newton Canoe Rental, Van Buren, Mo. 63965. The Current is also easily floatable by cartopper and john-boats.

MAINE'S ALLAGASH RIVER

For 92 miles the nation's first official Wild River carves a breathstakingly beautiful chain of rivers and lakes through the rugged Maine woods. Some 5000 sample it yearly, half making the whole trip and the others portions. This is the Allagash, probably the most famous float river in the East.

Renowned for its brook trout fishing, the other qualities that most quickly characterize the Allagash are solitude, some hairy white water, moose ducking their heads among lily pads, and everywhere the sharp-pointed pines in the background. Public campsites line the route.

The Allagash divides conveniently into two sections. The southern part offers access via several points to four large lakes and a side trip upstream six miles to Allagash Lake (no airplanes allowed here). This section is made-to-order for beginning family canoeists.

The northern section is more rivery and contains nine miles of rapids generally considered beyond the beginner's ability. However, a private timber company road can be used to skirt this part. Then resume the river travel via smaller lakes and the free-flowing stream itself to the take-out point at Allagash Village.

Since many of Maine's rivers are shallow and rocky, one will meet the canoe pole here. The metal-pointed poles are used to stop or slow the canoe going downstream or to push her up. The Maine guide is also a tradition unto himself. An L. L. Bean checked shirt and suspenders are required for admission. One will meet plenty of them on the Allagash, although a guide is not required. Here are canoes only, by regulation. Motors to 10 hp are okay.

The State Park and Recreation Commission, State Office Building, Augusta, Maine 14330 has an excellent free guide to the Allagash. Ask also for another brochure, *Maine Canoeing,* which lists all the water trails in the State.

There are several outfitters in the area. Two top ones are Allagash Outfitters in Millinocket, Maine, and Sanders Store in Greenville, Maine.

Special Note: If one wonders why some back country guides get that way, one of the streams emptying into the Allagash is the Chemquassabamticook River. Pronouncing names like that would make anyone a mite teched!

CHAPTER NINE

The Happy Canoe Trip

The experience of one large outfitter is that wilderness canoe-ists tend to fall into two categories: youths from 15 to 20 and professional people, or individuals with pressure-type employ-ment, mostly over 40 who want to get away from it all.

Canoeing is the easiest, and in many ways the best way to escape the rat race. But one should do his homework well. For instance, the following advice is for the advanced canoeist as well as the tyro.

Canoe trips that involve rivers require absolutely certain knowledge of the areas involved, unless one is really exploring. Also the stage of water must be taken into account. Unless one is a white-water expert, stay off any river even approaching flood state.

Approach rapids with extreme caution. One can get sucked in and forced to run them. Instead, land, look over the rapids from shore, and then decide—portage, line, or shoot. Description maps list all danger points, which is all to the good as portages can be surprisingly hard to find even on well-traveled routes. Look for them, along what looks like the easiest going, near the beginning of bad water.

In Canada especially, some smallish rapids have no portages because natives run them with ease. Don't be tempted beyond one's capacities, however. If one doesn't like what he sees, he should at least line down.

Consider weather when pitching camp. Watch out for quick river rises that can make sandbar or bottom camps dangerous. Too, an open ledge with a lovely view won't be so attractive if a gale blows in. Always overturn and tie the canoe down at night.

Cover packs and gear with a tarp at night and during the day when away from camp. Small plastic tarps are good on which to spread out cooking gear, by the way. The wide bottom of the canoe itself, blocked level, makes an appealing table.

When portages are well maintained, try the one-and-a-half portage. The first man carries the heaviest pack. The second man brings the canoe and a light pack. At the halfway point, each exchanges his load and then returns to bring the rest of the outfit. The way this works out, both men carry a 1½ load.

Camp early. Gather firewood and make everything as livable as possible. Then fish within easy paddling distance during the prime evening hours. Back at camp a match sets the pre-laid fire going, and one enjoys a refreshing cup while loons serenade and the cook puts the chow on the table.

Never plan any canoe trips that include any sizable amount of upriver travel unless one can use outboard power.

Beware of animals, especially if camp is left unattended. A black bear can devastate an outfit, two raccoons wreak havoc, and even a porcupine damage any salt-encrusted object such as a sweat-soaked paddle or even a wooden canoe itself.

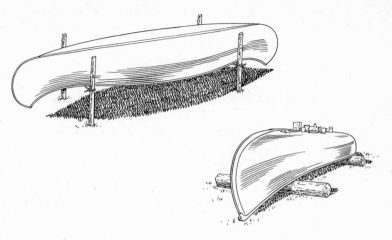

When nothing better's available canoe bottoms can serve as picnic tables.

If one's primary purpose is fishing or hunting, where one will be frequently returning to camp after dark, get a lightweight Dutch oven and let it cook dinner while the owners play.

COMMONEST CRUISING MISTAKES

Probably more unpleasant experiences befall the canoeist from the North's viciously biting insects than from any other cause. Brutal flies periodically run even moose into the water. Elsewhere mosquitoes can be actually deadly. In many places gnats drive people frantic. The defense? Plenty of bug dope such as Cutter's, the Pentagon's basic Deet, or OFF. It is also not a bad idea to carry an anti-itch lotion for bugs that do get through. If long portages through northern woods are ahead, all hands should be issued headnets.

Second to a mistakened lack of bug defense is not doing one's homework. One should be familiar with the route. This requires study.

The uninitiated tend to measure the success of a cruise by the distances traveled. Beginners' plans are generally too ambitious. Take a slow pace and enjoy it. Count at least one day in five as a weather day when prudence will dictate staying put.

Plan on oddball weather. If it doesn't snow, downpour, blow up a tornado or freeze, the canoeist should consider himself fortunate. Be prepared. Remember that one can take clothes off but can't add them if they're home in a closet. The sanest canoeing axiom everywhere is, "Hope for the best, but prepare for the worst."

One veteran canoe outfitter says that the beginner's most common mistake is failing to match trips to his abilities as an outdoorsman. Routes vary in the skills and stamina demanded. Study can put one in true tune with ambition, experience, and physical condition.

The commonest cruising accidents come from falls and cuts. Falls occur on rocks that are as slick as ice with moss or slime. A sprain, pulled muscle, or even a bad bruise can pose problems when one is dependent on brawn to move the canoe. Too, be wary of the axe. Pleasurable as it is to heft and handle, it still remains an unfamiliar instrument to most and is the cause of most camp cuts. Some camps make a rule that anyone chopping or splitting wood do so kneeling. That way there is no chance the axe can glance into a foot or leg. For those days when one is traveling out of the reach of a doctor, carry Stackpole's handy little *Being Your Own Wilderness Doctor* by E. Russel Kodet, M.D., and Bradford Angier.

CANOE CRUISING NECESSITIES

Everything starts with the canoe. One must learn the already discussed canoe skills; how to paddle it, turn it, capsize, and right it. Lakes, although in some ways the most perilous of all waters, are the easiest. Then the canoeist graduates to river skills. He learns to read rapids, run some simple ones, how to line a canoe up or down them, the basics of poling, and how to lift a canoe and carry it. None of this is very difficult, and just studying this book and practicing a bit, will accomplish it all.

Next come the simple camp skills. Today's "pop" tents fall in that category. They pop into shape; need no fancy poles or supports. This is the kind the usual canoeist wants (there are numerous brands) as then he won't be dependent upon trees and can make camp on river sandbars, on barren but bugless points, and among rocks. And they'll stand through high winds.

Speaking of rocks brings to mind a trail mattress. The new foam kinds are as comfortable as the older air varieties, but either will suffice. If one is young and full of beans, and in real wilderness, he can even make a bed of evergreen boughs. Use only those that can be broken off by hand, insuring the youngest and springiest of the lot. On these goes a sleeping bag. If one is headed north, this should be a good one. Expect Ontario's summer temperatures, for instance, to hit the 40's.

Then comes the need for someone in the party to master the very undemanding skill of learning to build an open wood fire in wet weather or dry, and how to cook over it. The three B's of canoe cooking used to be beans, bannock and bacon, but freeze-dry foods have classified that chestnut with the dinosaurs, at least in handily nearby waters. Still, to deny one's self the fresh fish fries, and (if one doesn't have to portage it too much) the pleasures of a dutch oven that makes dinner while one plays, is foolish. Be assured, too, that the woods will instill magic in those steaming hot biscuits or, baked for the fun of it, sourdough bread. Carry a good, basic, outdoor cookbook such as Stackpole's *Wilderness Cookery* by Bradford Angier.

The last but not the least important thing one should know about is maps; that is, canoe maps. All the famous canoe

rivers, indeed, almost every suitable river in this country and
Canada and Alaska is the subject of a study that lists its every
characteristic. In traditional canoe country, lakes are joined
by rivers and portages extend in every direction. The maps will
list alternate routes through the region, describing distances
and suggested lengths of time for traveling them. One should
never run any river he does not personally know without first
having studied a map of it. Coupled to the particular map will
be a knowledge of rudimentary navigation. Many lakes and
some river tributaries, such as those on the great Mackenzie,
are confusing. One should at least be able to hold a crude
compass course and know how to estimate time and distance.

That's all there is to it. Of course, as with everything, skill
is the Balm of Gilead. After all, a real woodsman can weather
a blizzard armed only with a match and for the best of everything an axe. On the other hand, plenty of poor souls have
huddled miserably amid expensive equipment, soddened by
storm or driven frantic by insects. Get in that homework.
If one goes to Ely, Minnesota, the jumping-off spot for the
Quetico-Superior canoe area, the outfitters will tell him that
a full quarter of their customers delight in the open spaces
without ever having camped or even having been in a canoe
before. Fortune favors the bold.

THREE WAYS TO START

There are three ways, really, for the would-be canoeist to get
his feet wet. Plunging in like the above, appealingly adven-
turous as it is, happens to be the worst. One can be burned
badly. If one is a loner, read the books, look and learn, and
head off with the wife and kids maybe an inch at a time. Float
a nearby stream and cook lunch, then dinner, ashore. Stay
overnight when the weather smiles. Expand one's horizons
along with accumulating experience. A fine alternate method
is to join a canoe club and paddle off with them on trips they

organize on a near-continuous basis. One will then have all the advice and help needed, plus the pleasure of making new friends.

One final point should be covered; the reason for going. All travel is an adventure because none of it is fully predictable. No matter how well one plans and prepares, zowie! In from left field comes the unexpected. But running a river is adventure of a different and more intense nature. It is at such drastic variance with everything in the individual's ordinary life today. At a stroke it simplifies existence to a dramatic degree. Gone are gadgets, business deals, assembly lines, parking tickets, bosses to please, bills, jangling telephones, traffic jitters, and mind-numbing television extravaganzas. Suddenly they're all behind. Then, in taking on this river, one has accepted the challenge of one's self. Safety and comfort depend on the individual alone. No others will be along to help the wilderness voyageur.

The simplicity of canoeing very soon reawakens lost senses. Natural beauty will show shyly at first, then engulf one. The very stars, such as Ursus Major and vital Polaris, will assume importance. An ice-cold drink of water will become an experience. One will rediscover conversation and the fact that people, after all, are happiest entertaining, exploring, and sharing themselves. Spend two weeks canoeing, and a tune on the harmonica or a voice raised in quiet song sounds like a symphony.

Rising to the challenge of one's self will do something more. Eric Severeid, the TV news personality, went on a long canoe adventure as a youth of 17. He has never forgotten it. Nor will one's own days on the lakes and rivers march off to obscurity. If one is lucky, many trips will merge in and out as time blurs memory. But one will never forget those warming dawns when he threaded his way along canoe waters armed only with a frail craft, a scrap of fabric, and his own skill.

CANOE CLUBS

Big Daddy of all the canoe clubs in North America is the American Canoe Association, lately in a resurgence of activity under the leadership of Tom Cooper. Address all correspondence to the executive secretary, at this writing Joan Mason, 4260 East Evans Avenue, Denver, Colorado 80222. To join the some 2000-strong membership list costs $6, for which one receives an annual yearbook listing all members, a directory of local canoe club affiliates and chairmen to write for information on the various ACA divisions such as sailing and cruising and whitewater racing, plus a magazine that keeps one current on all canoe activities. Subscription costs for non-members is $3.50.

Second to ACA is the United States Canoe Association, Charles Moore, President, 6338 Hoover Road, Indianapolis, Indiana 46260. Dues are $5 yearly. They, too, publish a magazine-newsletter.

Another club of importance is the American Whitewater Affiliate, Ed Alexander, President, 6 Winslow Avenue, East Brunswick, New Jersey.

OUTFITTERS

Unless one is unusually lucky there probably won't be a sporting goods store nearby that carries a truly representative selection of the specialized camp and cook gear the starting canoeist needs. Even if there is one, the buyer should compare goods and prices against those of a good mail-order firm.

One firm specializing in camping and outdoor gear is Morsan, 810 Route 17, Paramus, N.J. 07652 where, for example, nearly 200 tents and tarps are displayed in their main store. Wide selection, fair prices, and the fact that much of their service includes helpful advice on tents, packs, foods, etc. makes Morsan outstanding.

Another fine outfitter is mountain-climbing-and-European-oriented Trailwise on the opposite coast which offers much exotic as well as local super-light gear and an excellent freeze-dry food selection. Address Trailwise, 1615 University Avenue, Berkeley, California 94703 for catalogs.

The long-established firm of L. L. Bean, Inc., open to sportsmen 24 hours a day, is a traditional canoe supplier with emphasis on clothing but with much other excellent and practical gear. Spring and Fall catalogs are free, and there is the additional attraction that most items are sent postpaid. Just address L. L. Bean, Inc., Freeport, Maine 04032.

There is only one Herters, Inc., Waseca, Minnesota 56093, and their 650-odd page catalog selling for a dollar comes as close to being the bible of the outdoors as anything.

Three West Coast outfitters specializing in down sleeping bags and clothing, as well as elegant sportsmen's garb, offer canoe-applicable gear, too. All mail free catalogs. They are:

> Norm Thompson, 1805 N.W. Thurman Street, Portland, Oregon 97209.
> Chet Rice, Managing Owner, The Smilie Company, 575 Howard Street, San Francisco, California 94105.
> Eddie Bauer, Box 3700, Seattle, Washington 98124.

Excellent, too, and manufacturing much of their own equipment, is the Colorado Outdoor Sports Co., 1636 Champa Street, Denver, Colorado 80217. This is the concern that has taken over the famous Gerry Cunningham designs.

THE ALL-IMPORTANT MAPS

One of the most extraordinary mail-order houses in the country is Ohio Canoe Adventure, Box 2092, Sheffield Lake, Ohio 44054. Owners Reece and Marcy Fabbro have personally canoe-cruised over 5,000 miles, sell 1,000 canoes a year from their 7-day-week-open store (the coffee pot is always on, says their literature) and have written literally thousands of letters to compile what is unquestionably the most comprehensive source of canoe maps and literature ever assembled in one spot. Called *100,000,000 Miles of Canoe and Hiking Routes,* it includes a detailed river analysis of almost every major river, park and forest system in this country and Canada, plus all books that detail canoeing in various states, and what must be close to every book in print on canoeing, camping, and backpacking. The guide sells for a dollar. No serious canoeist should be without it.

The Fabbro river analyses are aimed at detailing the full recreational opportunities of each river and lake system. Where applicable, alternate canoe trails are listed in the same areas. In each, mileages, access points, float times, degree-of-water-difficulty ratings, danger points, water quality, fishing potential, suggested camp sites, and various other items of interest are detailed. Individual maps sell for $1.50 to $4, depending on length and complexity.

While the Fabbro analysis would be sufficient for most semi-wild rivers in this country, if heading into deep wilderness one should have topographical maps of the area he plans to cruise. In Canada, write the Map Distribution Office, Dept. of Mines and Technical Survey, Ottawa, Ontario. In the U.S., the Geological Survey, is the source. Write the Distribution Section, U.S. Geological Survey, 1200 South Eads St., Arlington, Va. 22202 re maps of areas east of the Mississippi River; their corresponding office at Federal Center, Denver, Colorado 80225 for maps of areas west of the Mississippi River. Costs are minimal, but topo maps are so detailed that quite a few may be needed. One would be hard pressed to amass over $10 worth, though.

Note among literature needs the ACA pamphlet listing free river information put out by state agencies. Many contain excellent maps. Also, no canoe cruiser should be without the Stackpole book. *Traveling The Water Trails of America* by Robert Colwell, which contains extensive descriptive detail on numerous American canoe waterways in all sections of the country, where to rent equipment, etc.

RENTALS

It is not even necessary to outlay for canoe, tent, sleeping bag, and cooking pots and pans to cruise the wilderness. In most popular canoe areas all gear can be rented. Ads listing outfitters there appear in the backs of the big hunting and fishing magazines.

Grumman Boat, Marathon, N.Y. 13803 will send free a list of dealers renting their canoes. One or more of these can be expected on every popular canoe stream.

Portage Stores Suppliers, Canoe Lake Post Office, Ontario, rents gear for use in Canada's famed Algonquin Park. And if really remote wilderness travel is one's bag, the 300-year-old Hudson's Bay Company rents canoes for travel across Canada's northlands. Ask for the U-Paddle Canoe Rental Service brochure, Hudson's Bay House, Winnipeg 1, Manitoba.

Rental costs vary but are generally modest. Figure about $10 per person per day if everything is hired. A canoe alone rents for around $8 per day.

CANOE TRIP COOKERY

Know all about hanging pots from Z sticks, banking reflector bakers, and all that tricky woods-cooking stuff? For short trips, especially when there will be portages, forget it.

Quite literally, to eat handsomely today along canoeing waters the only things one has to know is how to boil water and count. Freeze-dry foods are responsible for the big change.

Whole meals, breakfasts, lunches, steaks, beverages, and soups are packed in a dry state that keeps indefinitely without refrigeration. Since weights are ⅓ to ¹⁄₂₀ of the original, the new foods are joys on portages. Too, boatmen like the non-refrigeration bit.

Here's a sample one-day freeze-dry menu. Breakfast: orange juice, eggs with bacon bits, oatmeal with milk and sugar, coffee, tea and cocoa. Weight 31 ounces, cost $3 for four servings. Lunch: Why not have tuna salad with crackers, plus chocolate milk? Weight 20 oz., serves four, $3.50. Dinner puts cooked chicken in sauce with potatoes, peas, and carrots on the canoe bottom. Weight 4½ oz., serves one, cost $2.25.

To cook these just break open the package, pour in boiling water, wait 60 seconds (but no more, as the water can steam and dry the food) pour off excess, and everything is ready to eat. With cold foods obviously one adds cold water.

There are some disadvantages. Cost is high. Most meats do not taste like fresh meat, although they are as good as in TV dinners. The vegetables, fruits, beverages, and soups are the best. Bread and biscuit mixes are excellent. Puddings and gelatins are good. Of the meats, Wilson's beef patties and pork chops are the most popular.

There are other new ways for the canoeist. Frozen meats will stay that way for days at a time in a cooler in which a block of dry ice is kept. Wrap the ice in a newspaper.

Traditional canoe cooking has always been heavy on flour including prepared types like Bisquick, bacon (for cooking grease) oatmeal, powdered milk and eggs, and rice. Cabbage is a fresh vegetable that keeps well. Go heavy on cheeses, crackers, nuts, and dried fruits. Dried beef is an old favorite. It goes well with a variety of dishes and can be eaten separately as a snack. One will need snacks, too, as appetites grow in the fresh air and energy-expenditure.

Take plenty of sweets; jams, puddings, jellies, and syrups for flapjacks. No canoeist can exist for long without flapjacks. Canned meats, beans, and easy meals like canned spaghetti, hashes, and stews are traditional camp cooking favorites. How much tinned stuff one carries will depend on the amount of portaging. Another 100 pounds of food hardly can be noticed if one is paddling.

What the cook has to do is plan well in advance what's going to be served every day at every meal. Most books on canoe camping include several suggested menus, and Ohio Canoe Adventures include one with map orders. Get such a menu and personalize it. If one brings too much, remember Nessmuck's famous story. He was a go-light and said he hollered at a friend for carrying a bunch of food jars into the wilds, but made up for it by helping the fellow eat the contents. The best treatise on traditional canoe cooking, complete with menus, is offered by the ACA at 20¢ each. Ask for *Camp Cookery I & II*.

Freeze-dry foods can be had from various sources, including the nearest local supermarket. A mail-order firm specializing in freeze-dry and offering considerable variety is Stow-A-Way Products, 103 Ripley Road, Cohasset, Massachusetts 02025 (617-383-9116). Owner Bill White is very helpful. A free catalog can be had for the writing.

Another excellent firm specializing in pre-assembled meals and other freeze-dried and dehydrated foods is Chuck Wagon Foods, Micro Drive, Woburn, Massachusetts 01801. Their well-tested products are sustaining and enjoyable, as well as light, compact, and efficiently packed. Both the president of this concern and its plant manager are alert to canoeing needs.

TRIP EQUIPMENT LIST

For extended wilderness canoe trips several thousand people have used this list as a check list. One can therefore be sure it includes everything he'll need. If a more modest trip is planned, some items can be left behind. If several canoes travel together, many items can be shared jointly.

For the Canoeist

Two or 3 large waterproof packs, preferably with back frames if extensive portaging is expected. These house bulky items like tent, sleeping bags, food, and cooking gear.

One individual waterproof pack for each individual to hold personal clothing and equipment, such as lunch, drinking cup, powdered drink mix, snacks, toilet paper, sunglasses, and bug dope.

One small pack for all fishing gear except rods.

Rod case to hold all rods.

Waterproof gadget bag to keep loose items in place.

Tent with mosquito net; poles and pegs if needed.

Compass. Get a kind with the North indicator plainly marked.

Maps and description of route in plastic case.

Wristwatch, preferably waterproof.

Matches in waterproof case. Perhaps a lighter with extra fluid and flints.

Good sheath knife such as a Randall (eat with it, too) and an army-type knife with multiple blades and gadgets.

Flashlight with spare batteries and bulb.

One hundred feet light braided nylon cord.

Sleeping bag. Use a down liner if hot and cold nights are expected.

Air or foam mattress.

Two pairs trousers, one short if weather so indicates.

Two light shirts, at least one long-sleeved.

Two wool shirts or sweaters.

Parka or flotation jacket.

Knee pads.

Two sets underwear (one long if cold weather is anticipated).

2 pairs shoes (one moccasin-type short boot for camp).

4 pairs wool socks in assorted weights.

Pajamas (flannel if cold weather).

3 bandana handkerchiefs (make good sweat bands).

Leather belt.

Swim trunks.

Sunglasses with cord to prevent loss.

Sun hat.

Sunburn cream in plastic container.

Headnet for north woods, insect repellent in generous supply, anti-itch lotion, rubber bands to close trousers and shirt cuffs.

Lightweight rain suit with hood or hat.

Soap and soap dish.

Washcloth.

Small Turkish towel.

Toothbrush and paste.

Razor and blades. A windup or battery-electric shaver is even better.

Comb and steel mirror. Scissors for haircuts and beard trims.

Toilet paper.

Women's personal items.

Aspirin, lip cream, favorite medications, salt and Halazone or iodine tablets, 2 dimes.

Sewing kit, safety pins, buttons, heavy thread and needles to repair tent.

Fishing tackle and/or hunting firearms.

Hunting or fishing licenses; fire or camp permits.

Logbook and pencil or ballpoint pen.

Camera and film in waterproof bag.

For the Canoe and Motor

Three paddles.

Approved life jacket (not cushion type) for each individual.

Bow and stern lines for each canoe; $\frac{3}{16}''$ polypropylene rope at least 100 feet long.

Spare spark plug, plug wrench, and shear pins if motor is used. If running rocky rivers or lakes, use new plastic prop.

Bailing implements.

A basic repair kit, including, as may be needed, 25 feet light seizing wire, 1 roll new super-stick and super-strong fabric tape such as air and heat duct tape, epoxy glue, pliabond-type glue (for canvas), assortment of screws and nails and light bolts, adjustable wrench, pliers with wire cutters, piece emery cloth.

For canvas canoes: 2 x 3-foot piece canvas, pliabond-type glue, and copper tacks.

With aluminum or good fiberglas canoes, pound dents flat, close punctures with fabric tape.

For the Camp

Food. Don't forget condiments.

Nested cooking pots, griddle, reflector oven, Teflon ™ skillet-cooking grill, metal or collapsible pail.

Can opener, scouring pads, paper dish towels.

Cups, plates, cutlery.

Lightweight nylon tarp. Has multitude of uses.

Lightweight entrenching pick-shovel.

Folding saw.

Two axes, one with flat driving face, and sharpening stone or file.

Medicine kit and the handy-size Stackpole book, *Being Your Own Wilderness Doctor*.

*   *   *

Bon voyage!

CHAPTER TEN

Canoe Camping

The camping one does with his canoe can embrace some of life's most unforgettable hours, a reason for going about this in the most advantageous way possible.

Because of sunlight while actually camped, plus the fact that the country on that side is actually the more open, select a north bank whenever feasible.

There are two reasons for camping at least a dozen feet above the water level whenever this is possible. For one, such a site will be relatively safe from flooding, and a long river, especially, can lift dramatically in minutes, even when the local weather is serene, because of a storm nearer its source. Secondly, there is the matter of dew. The long streamers of mist that lift several feet above water at night can soon dampen equipment, sleeping bags, and canoeists who camp within their reach. A high camp, then, will in fair weather ordinarily be a dry camp.

DITCHING FOR DRAINAGE

In this connection, make as sure as possible that the spot has good drainage in case it rains. In any event, stay away from gullies that may become watercourses during storms. An otherwise good site can be ditched, of course. Just run a furrow along the upsides of tent and duffle so as to lead any rain away from them.

A channel two or three inches wide and deep can be made with the back of the camp axe or even with a sharp stick. If this groove is in the way of foot traffic as it may be by the tent door or if the soil crumbles easily, the drain's utility can be maintained by filling it loosely with pebbles.

With camps on a slope, water will, of course, have to be shunted only from the upper sides. If one is camped on sand or in forest so carpeted with vegetation that moisture sinks into it almost immediately, no ditching at all may be necessary.

VIEW, SPACE, BREEZES AND SAFETY

There's nothing like waking up with the first bright rays of the sun slanting in through the tent door, and as for the view, with all the choice there is on the lakes and rivers of this continent, it should be magnificent.

When waters are open for canoeing, flies and mosquitoes are also apt to be rife. For this reason it's generally most comfortable to camp in the open, where breezes from the water will keep a large proportion of such pests away.

Too, there are ordinarily enough good camping spots available so that it won't be necessary to pick a site that is too cramped. For one thing, the campfire should not be kindled too near tent and equipment. Sparks are then too apt to turn everything to ashes.

It does not pay to take chances with fire on any score.

Never kindle one on inflammable ground, such as that made up largely of decomposed and living vegetation. Fire will sometimes eat deep in such footing. An individual may think he has put it out, but often it may not be entirely extinct. Unseen and unsuspected, it may smolder weeks and months underground. It may lie nearly dormant during an entire winter. With the warmth and the increasing dryness of spring, it may regain fresh vigor until one hot day a strong wind causes it to grow into a roaring, exploding, devastating forest fire.

Before leaving camp for more than a few minutes in a potentially dangerous area, put out that fire. Saturate it with water. Stir the ground around and beneath it, working and soaking ashes and dust into mud. Dig around it until certain that no root nor humus will lead the blaze away like a fuse. Feel with the hands to make certain that all heat has been safely diminished. Examine the vicinity for any activity resulting from sparks and snapping embers.

Especial precaution must be taken in some country when a dutch oven is used. In a few areas, particularly during dry seasons, this handy shallow kettle with its rimmed cover should not be used at all except when one remains on the spot. Make certain, in any event, that the oven is buried in mineral soil and that no combustible material of any sort, be it roots or decaying forest litter, is near enough to begin smouldering.

TREE HAZARDS

Birches are substantial trees, and they often grow along lakes and streams, furnishing safe and beautiful camping spots. Avoid all trees that may fall or whose heavy branches may give away unexpectedly. This happens all the time in the living forest although, of course, the danger is most pronounced in wind or storm.

Small spruce, cedar, pine, fir, and the like also furnish welcome protection against gale and rain in a lot of canoe country, and in the unlikely circumstance that one is blown over no great harm will be done.

FOR SAFE DRINKING WATER

It is frequently possible on canoe trips to camp beside a small stream that is sparkling down from unsettled back country, and there can be the drinking water. However, even in such a circumstance it will not be possible, short of laboratory tests, to rely on such water's being safe. Even when a mountain rill cascades through untouched wilderness fastnesses, the rottening carcass of a winter-killed deer may be awash a few yards upstream.

The folklore that any water a pet dog will drink is pure enough for his owner is unfortunately as baseless as it is charming. Even the fact that local inhabitants may assert that a water source is pure may mean, instead, that they have built up an immunity or that because of long familiarity, they cannot believe that the water is tainted. A domestic water supply used by the inhabitants and guests of a Montana ranch for some two decades was found to have been infecting not only the present but the previous owners with tularemia. The germs of this, it so happens, can be carried to water by pets such as dogs, by domestic animals such as pigs, and even by the hardest working beavers though they themselves may seem to be completely healthy.

Taking a chance with drinking water in a town or city is, in one respect, a lot less dangerous than subjecting one's self to a minor fraction of similar risk along a wild stream where medical assistance can be days away. The only safe procedure is to assume that all water is impure until it has been proved otherwise, positively and recently.

Water can be rid of germs by boiling it for five minutes at sea level and for an additional minute for each 1,000 feet of elevation. This not only applies to water that is actually drunk. It is equally applicable to water in which the toothbrush is dipped, water in which dishes are washed, water used in cooking except when this is kept at a high enough temperature for a sufficient time to assure purity, and even water used with the strongest alcoholic beverages. Alcohol does not purify water.

Boiled water, as everyone knows, tastes flat because air has been driven from it by heat. Air, and at the same time taste, can be restored by pouring the cooled water back and forth between two utensils or by shaking it in a partially filled jar or canteen. Or if one is in a hurry and has salt, it is common practice to add a pinch of that.

One can purchase at most sporting goods and drug stores for about fifty cents a small two-ounce bottle containing 100 halazone tablets. Since their purifying action depends upon the release at the proper time of chlorine, these should be fresh. In other words, pass up surplus-store "bargains." The container should be kept tightly closed in a dry, dark place.

No purification of water by chemical means is as dependable as boiling, but two halazone tablets will ordinarily make a quart of water safe for human consumption in half an hour. If the water is muddy or especially questionable, it is sound insurance to double at least the amount of halazone and generally the time as well.

Chlorine-releasing compounds cannot be relied upon in semi-tropical and tropical regions, where water should either be boiled or, when this is not practical, treated with iodine. Ordinary tincture of iodine can be used as a water purifier. One drop of this fresh antiseptic, mixed thoroughly with one quart of water in the same manner as halazone, will generally make the water fit for human consumption in 30 minutes.

Both the amount and the time may be doubled if this precaution seems warranted.

Or use iodine water purification tablets, proved effective against all common water-borne bacteria as well as the cysts of endamoeba histolytica and the cercariae of schistosomiasis. Manufactured as Globaline by WTS Pharmaceuticals, Division of Wallace & Tiernan, Inc., in Rochester, New York, 50 iodine water purification tablets are packaged in a glass bottle with a wax-sealed top cap, obtainable by any drug store. Added to water, each tablet frees eight milligrams of iodine which acts as a purification factor. Each tablet will purify one quart of water. These tablets, too, must be kept dry, so the bottle should be tightly recapped after opening.

Care should be taken with all chemical purifiers to disinfect all points of human contact with the container, assuring that once the water is sterilized it will not be easily reinfected. If a jar or canteen is being used, replace the cover loosely and in the case of tablets wait several minutes so that they can dissolve. Then shake the contents thoroughly, permitting some of the fluid to spill out over the top and the lip of the holder. Tighten the cover then and leave it that way for the desired time before using any of the water.

Making A Filter

Water can be cleared by filtering, although this process will neither materially affect any dissolved minerals, nor will it assure purity. Water is contaminated by mineral and animal matter rather than by discoloring vegetable substances such as grass roots and dead leaves. The first two cannot be removed with any sureness by ordinary filtration.

The function of the makeshift filter is to clear water by straining solid materials from it. For example, one may be canoeing up near the Yukon border on the Sikanni River which is so muddy that some rivermen save time and effort by lugging kegs of drinking water with them. Filtration will serve instead, however.

A wilderness filter can ordinarily be made without too much difficulty, especially along sandy shores, by scooping a hole a few feet from the source of supply and using what water seeps into it.

Sweetening Water

On a particular day the paddler may make camp by a pond, perhaps in swamp or muskeg country, which has a disagreeable odor. It will be handy in such a contingency to know how to sweeten and purify water in a single operation.

This can generally be accomplished by dropping a few bits of charred hardwood from the campfire into the boiling pot. Some 15 minutes of simmering will then usually do the job. One can then skim away most of the foreign matter and finally either strain the water, as by pouring it through a clean cloth, or if time and utensils are no problem, by merely allowing it to settle.

Protecting The Environment

One goes canoeing not to prove he can survive but to enjoy himself. He should come back healthier than he was when he left. The matter of sanitation may sound like an arduous part of the journey. As a matter of fact, keeping the camp attractively healthy is simple once one learns a few of the tricks.

The ordinary fly is the common carrier of many disease germs, particularly typhoid. In the old familiar pattern, it lights on human or animal excreta and other refuse such as garbage. Then, carrying germs on its feet, it investigates what is going on in the dining department. All food, as well as every cooking and eating utensil, should be protected from flies in camp, either by keeping them in flyproof containers or by covering them with something such as cheesecloth. Fly sprays are also effective and are easily stowed in a canoe, but they should be kept away from food, dishes, and incidentally from open flame.

Special precautions should be taken along heavily traveled canoe routes and in camps that are continued in one spot for more than a few days. Latrines and garbage pits should be maintained, downstream from the source of drinking water, and these screened or darkened against flies. Deposits should be covered at once with dirt or ashes. The use of a disinfectant such as the inexpensive chloride of lime is also effective.

Garbage, including cans which should first be burned and flattened, should at least be placed in such a pit and covered with dirt, not just dumped on the ground. Bottles should be broken and then deeply buried. Exceptions take place along heavily frequented canoe trails where everything that cannot be diminished in the fire should be neatly brought back to civilization and there disposed of in regularly maintained containers.

On brief stops, when there is no call for a regular latrine, excreta should be deposited in a small hole, such as one dug by the heel well away from the water, and solidly and unobtrusively covered.

It is highly desirable that the wild places remaining on this busy continent be kept unspoiled and clean so that they can maintain, as long as possible, their attractiveness and their spiritual and aesthetic values. At home, some people have been accustomed to paying garbage men and caretakers to keep their surroundings clean and sanitary. Some others scatter their litter in neighbors' gardens and along streets and country roads where it may also be eventually removed.

Entirely too many forget that in wild terrain there is no one to clean up after them. As a consequence, scattered paper, cast-off clothing, rotting food, and other debris of every sort imaginable are too often seen. Along dry stream beds and across trackless deserts one can always tell these days where an automobile can penetrate by a trail of rusting beer cans and slowly disintegrating facial tissues.

Any canoeist can do worse than copy the woodchuck who is one of our cleanest animals, although most unjustly called a groundhog. His burrow never smells of anything but clover, grass, and clean earth. In it he has a blind alley, at the end of which he deposits all refuse and covers it with earth.

Dishwater, too, should not be emptied into a lake or stream or thrown about indiscriminately but, instead, tipped into a pit and covered with fresh earth. Washing dishes, incidentally, is really not too much of a chore on a canoe trip if one has some system about it and always cleans up immediately after a meal. With the cooking outfit, it will be helpful to include such items as a bar of laundry soap, two small tough dish-cloths, a little dish mop, and scouring pads which combine some hard substance such as steel wool with soap. While eating, have the largest kettle over the fire heating dishwater.

At the jumping-off place, buy a cheap dishpan and discard it when the trip is over. This will not take up much space if a model is selected in which other items can nest.

If one prefers, however, he can take along a small canvas wash basin. Such a seven-ounce affair that one of us has carried for years is four inches high and twelve inches in diameter, squashing down flat to pack. One can even get by with a square of plastic, digging a hole each time it is used and pressing the plastic within to serve as the washpan. If traveling particularly light because of portages, fill this with water while the meal is cooking, drop in a few pebbles for insulators, and using a bent green stick as tongs set in several large clean stones from the campfire to heat the water. The regular basin, however, is handier than either of these.

Every fellow, as he finishes his meal, scrapes his plate into the fire. When the cook is through with the frypan, fill this with water and put on the fire to boil. Do the same with any kettle containing the sticky residue of mush.

Down at the river or lake shore one will find clusters of growing grass, with mud or sand adhering to the roots. Or there may even be the scouring rush. Pull up a clump of either and use it to scour the outside of pots and also the interior and exterior of the frypans before washing them. Pans in which cereals like rolled oats have been cooked are particularly bothersome. If one will put a little square of butter or margarine in the water when preparing the cereal, it will make the pot a dozen times easier to clean.

If one has a pet aluminum pot whose exterior he wants to keep bright, coat the outside with a thick film of soap before placing it on the fire. All trace of black will then rapidly wash off. Eventually, most kettles get thoroughly darkened on the outside with soot, which sticks most tenaciously and which scarcely can be removed by anything short of sand or steel wool. But this soot does no harm whatsoever and even makes food in such a kettle cook faster. If one scours with muddy grass as suggested, very little will rub off on other things when packed. It is customary to have a canvas bag in which to store the nest of kettles and pans. This helps to keep them from blackening other articles in the outfit.

It has been the experience of a great many of the old sourdoughs in Alaska and the continental Northwest that when a utensil used for cooking meat is washed with soap, they get bad digestive disturbances akin to poisoning and that this ceases when such washing is stopped. One way to clean a steel frypan is to heat it very hot, then plunge it into cold water. If this does not remove all the dirt, then scrub it with sand and rinse it in clear boiling water. Another way of loosening grease is to fill the pan with water into which some wood

ashes have been dropped and allow the whole thing to come
to a boil beside the blaze.

BREAD ON A CANOE TRIP

On a canoe trip of more than a week, loaves of bread bought
at some store on the fringe of the wilderness soon become
stale, moldy, and unappetizing. Canoeists, working up fine
appetites with their paddles, enjoy hot and fresh bannocks,
biscuits, sourdough bread, corn pone, muffins, buns, rolls and
other such toothsome breadstuffs more than almost any other
class of foods.

These are all easily cooked over an ordinary wood fire
under the open sky. There is no need for a stove with a regu-
lated oven. For instance, there's bannock. Bakery bread is
balky when it comes to molding. Its air-filled softness is un-
reasonably bulky when it comes to packing, especially when
one considers that anyone can break himself off a chunk of
warm, steamy bannock after a few minutes of practically
foolproof effort.

The handiest method of readying bannock for a canoe trip
is to mix the dry ingredients before leaving. In fact, one can
make up a number of such batches at home, sealing each in
a small plastic bag. This mix has multiple short-notice uses.

The following basic bannock mix, given here in one-man
proportions, will stay fresh for six weeks or more along the
waterways of this continent if kept sealed, dry, and reasonably
cool:

  1 cup all-purpose flour
  1 teaspoon double-action baking powder
  ¼ teaspoon salt
  3 tablespoons oleomargarine

If this mix is being readied at home, sift the flour before
measuring it. Then sift together the flour, baking powder and
salt. Cut in the margarine with two knives, with an electric

mixer at low speed, or with a pastry blender until the mixture resembles coarse meal. For increased smoothness and nutrition, add two tablespoons of powdered skim milk for every cup of flour.

Place in plastic bags. Seal with a hot iron or with one of the plastic tapes. A large quantity can be made at once, then divided into one-meal proportions. Before using, it will be a good idea to stir the mixture lightly.

If compounding this mix in camp, do it with the ingredients at hand in the simplest way possible. Any solid shortening may be utilized if the mix is to be used within a short time. Such mix can be carried in a glass jar or just folded in wax paper.

DRY MIX PRODUCTS

For Hot Trail Bread   When the campfire is going and everything else is ready, quickly add enough water to the basic mix to make a firm dough. Shape into a long, thin roll no more than an inch thick. Wind this ribbon on a preheated green hardwood stick, the diameter of a rake handle, so trimmed that several projecting stubs of branches will keep the dough in place.

Hold the bannock in the heat, occasionally turning it, for a couple of minutes. Once a crust has been formed, the stick may be leaned between the fringes of the fire and some reflecting surface such as a log or rock for the some 15 minutes required to form a tasty brown spiral. Or just shove a sharpened end of the stick into the ground beside the fire and turn this holder now and then while readying the remainder of the meal.

For Frypan Bread   When ready to go, add to the basic mix enough cold water to make an easily handled dough. Form this into a cake about an inch thick. If crust is enjoyed, leave a doughnutlike hole in the middle. Dust the loaf lightly with flour so it will handle more easily. Lay the bannock in a warm, greased frypan. Hold it over the heat until a bottom crust forms, rotating the pan a bit so that the loaf will shift and not become stuck.

Once the dough has hardened enough to hold together, turn the bannock over or, with a campfire, prop the frypan at a steep angle so that the loaf will get direct heat on top. When crust has formed all around, the bannock may be turned around a few times while it is baking to an appetizing brown.

After one has been cooking frypan bread awhile, he will be able to tap the loaf and gauge the degree of doneness by the hollowness of the sound. In the meantime, test by shoving in a straw or sliver. If any dough adheres, the loaf needs more heat. Cooking can be accomplished in about 15 minutes. If one has other chores, twice that time a bit farther from the heat will allow the bread to cook more evenly.

For Drop Biscuits   Mix rapidly with enough water to make a soft dough. Drop by the spoonful atop a hot greased metal surface and bake in a very hot dutch oven or reflector baker for 10 to 15 minutes.

For Fruit Cobblers   Add to each basic proportion 1 tablespoon sugar, 1 well-beaten whole or reconstituted egg, and ½ cup reconstituted milk. Stir just enough to dampen all the dry ingredients. Fill greased muffin rings, improvised if necessary from aluminum foil, about ⅓ full. Bake in a hot dutch oven or reflector baker about 20 minutes. Eat at once. For a dessert, cook with a teaspoon of jam or marmalade atop each muffin.

For Shortcake   Add one tablespoon of sugar to each basic proportion to make half a dozen medium-size shortcakes, which will afford a pleasant change of diet in berry season. Mix with ⅓ cup of cold water to form an easily handled dough. Flatten this to ¼ inch and either cut squares with a knife or punch out ovals with a can top. Brush half of these with melted margarine. Cover each with one of the remaining pieces. Bake in a dutch oven or reflector baker. Serve hot with fruit.

For Flapjacks   Add ½ cup milk, with which a whole or dried egg has been stirred, to the basic proportion. Stir only enough to moisten the dry ingredients. Grease the frypan, which should be ready and hot, sparingly with bacon rind. Do not let the metal reach smoking temperatures. Turn each flipper only once, when the hot cake begins showing small bubbles. The second side takes about half as long to cook. Serve steaming hot with margarine and sugar, with berries, or with syrup.

For Dumplings   Stir ¼ cup of cold milk or water into the basic proportion. Have everything ready to go, for these dumplings should be cooked only eight or ten minutes, and then the meal should be served immediately. Have broth simmering above enough meat and vegetables so that the dumplings will not sink. Moisten a big spoon in the broth. Use it to place large spoonfuls of dough, apart from one another, atop the stew. Cover tightly.

After several minutes each dumpling can, if one wants, be turned carefully and speedily. Re-cover immediately and continue simmering until light and fluffy. Then serve without delay. If any dumplings remain for second helpings, place them in a separate hot dish so they won't become soggy.

For Coffee Cake   Stir three tablespoons of sugar into each basic proportion of the mix. Combine a scant ¼ cup milk with one egg, fresh or dried, and stir well into the mix. Pour speedily into a shallow greased pan. Sprinkle powdered instant coffee and sugar, as well as perhaps nutmeg and cinnamon, over the top. Bake in a hot dutch oven or reflector baker about 25 minutes. Delectable!

THE DUTCH OVEN

The dutch oven, especially adaptable to canoe trips unless there is to be an excessive amount of portages, will bake biscuits and bread deliciously both below and above ground. Heat the contraption first, setting the lid on a good solid fire and easing the pot atop that. When the pot is hot, the meal will be ready to go.

Say one wants to bake a mess of the previously described biscuits. Drop a blob of butter, margarine, lard, bacon drippings, or other edible grease into the pot and work it around a bit. While it is melting, ready the biscuits. Put them into the pot and plant this solidly and evenly above a bed of coals and ashes. Clang on the lid. Heap additional coals onto that. The fact that the lid has been preheated to a higher temperature than the pot should balance the natural rising tendency of heat sufficiently to cook the tops and bottoms of the biscuits evenly.

One can take a look after about ten minutes. If the biscuits are not already taking on a healthy tan, rake the accumulating cinders and ashes from the lid and substitute more live coals. Dutch ovens require a certain amount of cooking experience, but the biscuits should ordinarily be ready in a dozen or 15 minutes.

Bread, taking longer to bake, is better adapted to underground cooking. For this, start in the forenoon by digging a hole somewhat larger than the oven and filling it with a blazing hardwood fire. As a basic precaution, be sure this pit is in mineral soil, well away from roots and humus. When the blaze has burned down to coals, shovel or rake out about half of these. Set in the preheated and greased dutch oven with a big, round, possibly sourdough loaf (see *Wilderness Cookery* by Bradford Angier) bulging in it. Ease the oven around until it's setting evenly. Then move the embers and ashes back in until the utensil, except for its upraised bail handle, is hidden.

A certain amount of experience is helpful here, too. If it seems the coals are going to be too hot, insulate the oven with an inch or so of ashes. Then spend the afternoon getting enough trout or wild strawberries to go with those crusty hot slices that will be waiting at suppertime. Or maybe there will be a sizzling roast or a savory stew, almost whatever desired can be readied in this versatile cooker.

It's not that this old-fashioned oven, preferably made of cast iron, does not have its disadvantages. It is awkward and heavy to carry unless one is traveling in something such as a canoe. Furthermore, although it holds the heat, it will rust if not kept well greased. Other varieties, such as those made of aluminum, are both lighter and easier to keep clean. But they are for city stoves if anywhere. They don't even come close to getting the job done over outdoor fires.

What one wants for food along the farther canoe trails is a heavy, thick, cast-iron pot with a similarly rugged top, lipped to hold a ruddy bed of coals. If local dealers don't have one, write the Lodge Manufacturing Company in South Pittsburg, Tennessee. The model generally most satisfactory for small parties is 12 inches in diameter, 4 inches deep, and weighs 17 pounds. Models are also available eight, 10, 14, and 16 inches in diameter.

The dutch oven the canoeist gets should have squat legs both to keep the bottom safely above the otherwise scorching ardor of hot embers and also to anchor the utensil levelly. It will need a convenient handle by which the hot top can be lifted and a likewise easily manipulated bail by which the entire contrivance can be moved. Both these jobs can be performed with the help of a forked stick cut on the spot. A shovel is also handy. One of the husky, folding models available at surplus stores is convenient to carry.

Old-timers season their dutch ovens when they first buy them—and afterwards if they have been cleaned with a modern detergent—by boiling grease in them. Otherwise, the cast iron which is porous will give trouble in making the food stick. This is a sound precaution, too, with the heavy iron frypans so convenient to the canoeman.

CHAPTER ELEVEN

Canoe Days*

FIRST DAY

The train gave off great bellows of diesels and the clacking of decelerating wheels, and suddenly the silence of the woods descended on the four. Later they laughed about it, poo-poohed the little pits in the bottom of stomachs, the pockets of uncertainty, the what-have-we-got-ourselves-into feeling. Middle-aged Bert and Laurie Spiller were fairly new to canoeing. They'd made a few easy floats and had fished from a canoe, but tennis kept them in good shape and they anticipated no problems. The youngest of the four was Hank Stives, in his mid-30's and still steel-hard from football days. He'd never been in a canoe before but was a willing pupil of the fourth man, canoe-veteran Dr. George Honeywell. Honeywell

---

* Being a conjectural account of a possible 10-day canoe vacation today across a North Woods wilderness.

long ago earned his wood's Ph.D.: Camp Fire Club of America, ACA member for 50 years (he joined at age 10). His experience went back to times when a horse and wagon carried him and his father into the woods. He'd lead the expedition in the same relaxed fashion that he'd organized the trips and led the planning.

Now they sorted out the chaos the baggage car had made of their careful preparations. Everything had been meticulously stowed, but it came out in a jumble. The only comfort was it was all there. George had packed everything in six large bags and personally assured himself they were loaded. Six big bundles went aboard. Six big bundles sat between the Spiller's nearly new fiberglas canoe and Dr. Honeywell's dented, scarred, and patched Grumman standard aluminum number 27. Honeywell was proud of that 27.

He'd anticipated the sudden apprehension and self-consciousness. Down from the train trestle there was a broad grassy strip and a stand of alders. It was late in the afternoon, and Honeywell suggested they make camp there and get things straightened out, waiting until morning to push on. When everyone agreed the wise old woodsman did what every man who feels lonely in a forest should do. He built a fire.

A campfire is one of mankind's most formidable discoveries, and this one was no exception. All at once Laurie forgot her second thoughts and began digging in for her pots, pans, and food supplies. She'd appointed herself cook over the protests of the men. This was a vacation. They'd take turns. No, Laurie had insisted. Campfire cooking wasn't like home cooking. It was fun. Recently engaged bachelor Hank Stives volunteered that he'd better get some lessons in dish washing and garbage disposal, and that seemed to settle matters.

With the fire going, there was a need to decide where the tents were to stand. Spiller's brand new pop tent had been raised several times on the living room floor and took shape instantly. Honeywell's umbrella tent went up slightly slower, but it, too, reflected the changed way of the wilds. George said he'd felt like the cavalryman shooting his horse when he gave up his old canvas wall tent with its stakes and ridgepole. But the new self-supported tents of modern fabrics were so superior, he said, there simply wasn't any contest. The only thing they lacked was smell. Once you got the scent of treated canvas in your bones, you never completely got it out.

This was a shakedown night, but without knowing it little precedents were being formed that were to last the length of the trip. Laurie not only cooked but established herself in charge of the pots, pans, and supplies. George was the fireman. He built each campfire, gathered a wood supply, and now was busily ringing the little flame with rocks for the grill to sit on. Soon he would have Y sticks at either end to support pot holders.

Bert and Hank were fishing nuts. They'd met on a bass lake. They handled the camp chores: put up the tents, ditched them, rigged the flies, located the latrine site and dug a slit trench, lashed the canoes down, blew up the air mattresses, and laid out the sleeping bags. They worked fast and were soon off on the river, flyrods poking the shoreline for tomorrow's breakfast of brook trout.

In fact, it had been fish that provided the spark for the trip. Hank and Bert had learned of a lake that contained huge pike. They'd been talking of it at a party one evening when Doctor Honeywell got into the conversation. Flying into the lake had been explored and rejected as too expensive.

"Maybe we could canoe in?" suggested old-hand Honeywell. Soon, pouring over his topographical maps, he found that the four could put in at the railroad bridge, go down one large river, and then make a short portage to another smaller, swifter stream that emptied into the large lake. The lake was a real monster, and the thought was to make a permanent camp there for several days while the fishermen attacked the pike. After that it was a long ride down the lake and a two-day trip down its swift and often dangerous tributary to a small town where a car could be hired to transport them back to the city where their own automobile was parked.

Counting on, but not depending on fish to eat, Dr. Honeywell and Laurie had worked out an ingenious menu that centered around an inexpensive styrofoam cooler. A piece of dry ice wrapped in newspaper would keep fresh meats cold for a week, and since only one small portage was involved weight wasn't a consideration at this point. When the fresh meat was gone, freeze-dry and suitable lightweight grub would be used on the hardest part of the journey.

All by way of saying that as dusk drew the shadows long over the river, a two-inch thick steak was sputtering over the fire, sending out rapturous smells to mingle with the equally rapturous aroma of balsam. . . Steak, beans, fresh biscuits baked on the reflector, all washed down with coffee, started the adventure well.

SECOND DAY

George Honeywell had decided on a leisurely start. In fact, the whole pace was leisurely. There was going to be no need to rush or hurry on the trip, and George made especially sure that was true at the start. Knowing that it would take several days to become accustomed to the sleeping bags, a wake-when-you-please morning was decreed. It was actually 9 o'clock when the smell of bacon and brook-trout filets cooking smoked Hank out into the open.

The sun was hot and high when George sent the men off for suitable saplings to lay in the canoe, opened tarpaulins on top of them, and carefully stowed the gear. The Spillers set out ahead, and soon the others followed, Honeywell giving no

advice on paddling to his young friend, letting him sort out
the strokes by trial and error.

Lunch was a fast affair—a small fire made on a beautiful
sandy beach point. Freeze-dry soup for something hot, along
with peanut butter and jam spread on biscuits baked after
breakfast for the purpose, the whole washed down with hot
tea, made up the meal. They laughed at eating peanut butter
and jelly sandwiches as if they were children, but it was
delicious.

At four p.m. they found an island in the river and made
camp for the night. Again the camp chores seemed to do
themselves, and the fishermen were soon at it, although they
grumbled later at coming so far and catching only two little
trout. Despite their conditioning, the paddling affected them
all. Laurie yearned to relax stiffened muscles in a hot bath,
and the men's shoulders and arms ached. Hands, too, were in
poor shape. Bandaids went on over incipient blisters. All
agreed around the campfire, as drowsiness overtook them,
that another leisurely start was in order the next day.

THIRD AND FOURTH DAYS

It took them almost twice as long as they had planned to
reach the portage. It would eat into fishing time on the lake,
but pushing at this point with its threat of raw and blistered
hands, aching and possibly pulled muscles, was simply too
risky. The trip was supposed to be pleasant.

Otherwise, the four adapted well. They were all sleeping
like children. The combination of sparkling air, exercise, and
good plain food infused them with vigor. They had pork chops
the second night, a canned ham the third, with ham sandwiches from leftovers the next day. Ravenous appetites
gripped everyone. All, including Laurie, were eating like a
horse or, more aptly, like the bull moose they sent, startled
and snorting, out of the river the fourth afternoon.

FIFTH DAY

Nobody let a hint of it out at the time, but in the trip-rehashes everyone agreed the fifth day was the low point of the expedition. First, the portage was a nightmare. There was a trail, and indeed it was short. Trouble was it was almost completely overgrown. A half-day's axe work was required to clear it and this in the rain. They awoke to leaden skies and a light drizzle. The wetness brought out the bugs, and the North's black flies attacked. All liberally slopped on insecticide which quickly washed off because of a combination of sweat and drizzle. When the trail was cleared it was slippery and dangerous, steeper than it looked on the map.

It was four p.m. before they got everything to the end of the portage, and to make matters worse the smaller river offered a poor place to camp. No one relished the idea of pushing on, possibly having to make camp after dark, so they reluctantly pitched the tents at the portage.

Nothing went well. The fire that usually sprang instantly to life at George's command was stubborn. Laurie burned the laboriously transported fresh steaks. Hank went for a swim (because of the icy waters swift swims were the rule), slipped on a rock and badly bruised an elbow.

To top it off, even the night conspired to disturb them. At 3 a.m. a sudden crashing brought them all bolt upright, the men soon exploring the darkness with flashlights. It was an animal of some kind, a raccoon or perhaps a porcupine. (They didn't tell Laurie until she was safely back in her living room that they'd found, and carefully erased, the footprint of a black bear not eight feet from where she was sleeping! Apparently the bear had followed the food smell right into camp. When human scent filled its nostrils, the bear panicked and made a commotion getting away.)

SIXTH DAY

Rain continued to fall steadily. They held a council of war, and everyone agreed they should push on and put the camp of bad memories behind them. The rain wasn't as bad as expected. Ponchos and wide-brimmed hats kept the water off splendidly, and the current in the smaller river was much swifter. The feeling that they were making good time enthused all. Hank was favoring his arm, wisely not pushing it into even greater inflammation. About 11 a.m. George reached for his kit bag, studied the maps carefully, and called for a war council.

He suggested they confine themselves to the raisins and nuts Laurie always provided for snacks and push on ahead. At that rate they'd make the lake around 2 o'clock and would have time to set up a proper bad-weather camp, build Laurie a decent dry area in which to cook, and make a permanent camp for the several days that they planned to stay.

They found a site of such splendor that even the rain couldn't dampen their spirits. It was on an island bluff, looking down the lake and tucked under a mountain. Even with darkened skies it was majestic, and they turned eagerly to building the camp. Tents went up, and tarpaulins were opened. As Laurie fiddled with dinner (the ice box was getting low now), the three men worked to build a hemlock shelter over her. Axes had become as familiar as pens at home, and all accused George of cheating when he fished in his gear bag and fetched some nails with which to fasten the sapling framework to handy trees.

The rain came steadily down, but it mattered not. The lake was refreshingly warm after the rivers, and the men all disappeared with bars of soap. Laurie after dinner filled every pot with water, heated them, and retired to her tent for a bath.

The fire burned long that evening. They were re-learning

one of mankind's most fascinating pursuits, the exploration of others. Talk was long and deep, and the song of the rain drew them closer together. Poetry came out of their past. Bert had memorized the Rubyiat, and suddenly that hymn to life popped into his memory. The others listened spellbound to his soft recital of the bittersweet verses. The bookish doctor countered with a surprising offering. He was a Kipling nut, and soon light-brigade charges, Gunga Dins, and far-flung battle lines had them clapping and asking for more. It was outrageously late when they went reluctantly to bed.

SEVENTH DAY

The fishermen left at dawn despite still-falling rain. After a late and leisurely breakfast Honeywell's small bag produced several paperback books. He pulled one of the canoes under the tarpaulin fly to make a backrest and was soon absorbed. Laurie pulled on a poncho, donned a hat, and announced she would explore up a small stream that tumbled into the lake not far away. George cautioned her to stick to the brook so as not to get lost, and she was gone.

She returned for lunch with tales of a beaver pond she'd located and how she'd hid and watched the industrious animals fell a tree and drag it to the pond. Lunchtime came and went with no fishermen, and the afternoon slipped by. Laurie began to worry. Nonsense, George snorted. They'd found fish. That was what the absence meant. There was no way they could come to any harm unless they'd melt in the rain.

He was right. They came back with tales of monster pike bigger than they'd ever hoped for. Great huge fellows, they were, fabulous in their plentitude, splendid in their slashing strikes and leaping hard-fighting attempts at freedom. They had caught smaller walleye'd pike aplenty as well and had a stringer full to prove it. They'd gone ashore at lunch, the two happy anglers reported, filleted the fish, and broiled them on spits. They were so fabulously delicious that the rest of the string went to provide everyone's dinner along with coffee, beans, and bannock.

That night they made strategy. George Honeywell wanted a full day to run the lake and two days in which to tackle the fast white-water stretch. That meant they should leave tomorrow. The fishermen wanted to stay, pleading for at least one more day of such dreamed-of fishing. So what if they arrived a day late? So what, indeed.

The evening produced another surprise. Hank had a harmonica. He'd forgotten that he threw it in his ditty bag, but now out it came. They spent the evening singing. At first all joined in the old favorites, but soon Laurie's great knowledge of folk songs took over, and her lilting soprano filled the camp with tales of lovers torn asunder, foul deeds revenged, and cavaliers come a courting. It was late again when the incessant patter of raindrops lulled them to sleep.

EIGHTH DAY

Dawn came crisp and clear with bright sunshine and a brisk north wind. The fishermen left again at light. George went back to his book and Laurie back to her beaver pond. But the day didn't repeat itself. The fishermen were back early. They had good strikes, but the fabulous fishing of yesterday was no more, turned off by the shift of wind and weather.

While they ate lunch, Honeywell studied the wind and then said that he thought they could sail down the lake in the afternoon if they didn't want to fish. Immediately, this captured everyone's interest. Under his instruction saplings were cut and the two boats lashed together. Other saplings made masts, and a light tarp was stretched between these. Underway, they discovered the following wind blew them along far faster than they could paddle.

It was dusk when they reached a campsite near the river outlet, but they were so experienced now that the light of the campfire was all that was needed to make a comfortable camp. With the wind shift had come cold. They didn't tarry over the fire. The sleeping bags went into action early.

NINTH DAY

They broke camp at dawn, all eager to tackle the challenge of white water. Hands were hard now, muscles used to driving the boats. Honeywell explained simple white-water techniques, how to draw and push and set, the bow and stern paddler's responsibilities, how to respond to commands, and how to "read" the water. His audience was attentive. They'd seen on the maps three, possibly four, stretches of unknown and probably dangerous rapids, plus a good-sized waterfall.

The river had speed and strength far greater than the others, and they weren't surprised to find a well-worn portage at the first rapid. It was a long one, more than a mile. Had it occurred at the beginning of the trip it might have proved disastrous. As it was, low supplies had lightened loads, and muscles were stronger. The carry was a chore that absorbed four hours, but the brisk weather kept the fly dope in place. Laurie had a lunch of thick soup and freeze-dry hamburgers in sourdough rolls waiting for the men when the last load came over.

They decided to shoot the next rapids, first scouting it carefully from the high bank. There were canoe-killing spots, but a smooth path could be found the entire distance. Honeywell spelled it all out for them—how to come down the left, then cross at the fallen tree by drawing, then follow the deep water on the right shore. He and Hank went first, George shouting commands and Hank handling the bow as if he was born there. They were soon through and as a precaution took rescue ropes upstream and watched while the Spillers came down, shipping some water but without harm.

The falls proved to be spectacular, too fishable to leave behind. They portaged around them and made camp downriver far enough away from the powerful roar. Brook trout with seemingly insatiable appetites went after the anglers' flies, and under them the bottom seemed carpeted with walleyes. The doctor surprised everyone by breaking out a backpack rod and joining in the fun. Even Laurie couldn't resist such fishing. Walleyes and brook trout were on the menu that night, cooked and eaten only after darkness drove the four from the river.

LAST DAY

The worst rapids was as mean as any Honeywell had ever seen. The portage was rocky and treacherously steep. They lined the boats down. Even this proved difficult.

A bluff required one stretch to be conquered by the men swimming between two giant rocks, safely tethered on lifelines. It was tricky work, the current always trying to set the canoes spinning. They inched the boats down, keeping taut lines, taking plenty of time, and avoiding an accident or spill. They breathed a sigh of relief at the end, and over lunch Laurie made a suitable audience for recounting the many perils involved.

As if the river was willing to dish out the bitter as well as the sweet, the last white-water was exactly what a well-made rapids should be. It was long, almost two miles of fast, broken water. But it was safe. Even Laurie could see it had none of the snarl of the previous stretches. This water was dancing. And the path down it looked as if it had been designed by highway engineers.

They entered it eagerly and shot through the broken spots,

relishing the speed and the thrills. Different feelings arose now in stomach pits when a turn around a bend brought the take-out village into sight. This time regret, even dismay, showed on all their faces. They were exchanging the world of woods and water for one of asphalt and sidewalks—that it was a bad bargain they were making was uppermost in everyone's thoughts.

Soon they were speeding down a superhighway instead of a rapids, and the trip was behind. Like all such it would fade in memory, true enough. But canoe adventures never disappear. A little of them, the bad and the good, tag along always. A photograph, a water-marked page in a notebook, a note on a map, and there the moments would be again in all their intensity.